Cheerleading for Writers

Discover How Truly Talented You Are

Victoria Ichizli-Bartels

Victoria Ichizli-Bartels

Cheerleading for Writers
Discover How Truly Talented You Are
1st Edition

The sources of the quotations made in the book are given
in the same chapters as the quotes in the text.
ISBN:1978247575
ISBN-13:9781978247574

Optimist Writer
optimistwriter.com

For Marcy,
Thank you for the gift of cheering me through my first book and for believing in me.
This book is for you and all wonderful cheerleaders of creativity.

Table of Contents

Preface

Here is what I wrote in the acknowledgments to my first book, *The Truth About Family*:

"My dear friend, Marcy, Marcella Belson, was my main cheerleader through the whole process. She read the book chapter by chapter, asked brilliant and revealing questions, and requested more to read. That motivated me to keep on writing, which for a first novel is simply vital. Her eagerness to discover how the story developed left me no chance to give up. Although we haven't met in person yet, Marcy, you have become one of my dearest friends. Thank you with all my heart!"

When I tell the story (and I do it often) of how Marcy found me through my blog and how she cheered me through my first book and continued cheering through my other writing projects, I often hear the following words, "You are lucky to have a reader like this."

And I truly am!

I am also blessed by my very best friend, my niece, Mihaela Breum, who has been an extraordinary editor and beta-reader. Along with editing and brilliantly critiquing my first two books, she also pointed out many well-done parts in my writing, which showed me the direction to take. The same goes for my dear friend and writing teacher Menna van Praag,* my editors Alice Jago,** Leah Schneeflock,*** and Rob Bignell,**** and my other beta-readers and writer-friends from various writing groups and clubs. They critique without judging and, best of all, they tell me what they like.

More than five years ago, I stumbled upon something, without which I wouldn't have started blogging, wouldn't have met Marcy on the internet, wouldn't have met many of my wonderful and supportive friends from all over the world. Without this something, I wouldn't have written the many books I have to date, including the one you are holding and reading right now.

This something was a book. Its title is *Being Here: Modern Day Tales of Enlightenment* and it was written by Ariel and Shya Kane.

I first saw it when an online retailer generated a recommendation based on my previous orders of self-help and motivational books. After buying and receiving it, I resisted reading it for almost two years. But my sight kept being captured by the beautiful butterfly on its cover, and even by its spine when I tucked it between the other books on one of my bookshelves.

At some point, I surrendered and read it. I learned about a unique approach called Instantaneous Transformation developed by Ariel and Shya Kane***** (see references 1, 2, and 3 in the Section "Recommended Reading" at the end of this book). And with time, I learned and experienced the three revealing principles of this approach.

First, I realized that if I resisted something or tried to get rid of something – a thought, a habit, a person, a task, or anything else – I didn't get rid of it at all. This person or thing just kept on sticking around, dominated my life and often became overwhelming.

Then, I learned that I couldn't be anywhere else or anyone else at any given moment -- I could only be who and how I was (or wasn't), whether I liked it or not. And whether I judged my situation or not.

Finally, there was the Kanes' third principle – anything that I allowed to be exactly as it was without judging or trying to change it, completed itself in an instant.

As I read Ariel and Shya's books and articles, listened to their *Being Here* internet radio show, and participated in their live seminars, I experienced what it meant to let myself and others be just as we were. I discovered how to breathe and savour my life moment by moment, completely and freely. I came to understand what I truly wanted, what was my heart's desire.

Yes, reading *Being Here: Modern Day Tales of Enlightenment* was the moment when this beautiful journey I am now on began. It was a journey of curiosity about what was happening at any given moment of now and what could happen if I surrendered to my wishes and did what my heart called me to do, instead of what I *thought* others wanted me to do.

As I practiced transformation, being in the moment, I discovered again and again that kindness and honesty were mutually inclusive, not exclusive. This allowed me to start observing myself non-judgmentally, in my life and also in the process of writing, reading and self-editing what I had written.

This non-judgmental study of my writing and creative processes, the many discoveries I made along the way, the feedback I received from my friends and cheerleaders, and especially my interactions with Marcy, made me want to give this gift of cheerleading to others.

I realized that I couldn't possibly read all the first novels by all aspiring writers. So I came up with another idea of how to pay this gift forward. I decided to write a series of essays covering various topics of writing, publishing, and life, and how my cheerleaders have helped me discover pearls inside my writing and creativity.

This book is the revised, edited and improved version of the articles published on my website in a blog series between November 2015 and October 2016.

I hope you enjoy reading this book as much as I enjoyed writing it, and I hope it helps to boost your motivation and bring fun to your writing projects.

Resources referenced in this chapter:

* www.mennavanpraag.com

** www.alicejago.co.uk

*** http://leahschneeflock.com/

****

http://inventingrealityeditingservice.typepad.com/invent
ing_reality_editing/

***** www.transformationmadeeasy.com

Introduction (Part 1) –

We All Have Cheerleaders

Here is the result of an internet search for the word *cheerleader*:

- *"A member of a team that performs organized cheering, chanting, and dancing in support of a sports team at matches.*

- *An enthusiastic and vocal supporter of someone or something."**

We all need cheerleaders. We need motivators and supporters.

And we do have them.

Our parents were the first ones, even before we started to walk. Then came teachers and friends. And siblings too, even if we might have seen them as rivals when we were small.

I had and have many cheerleaders in my life.

My father started by naming me Victoria, later telling my mother that he wanted this name for me because I was his victory.

My mom raised the "jumping bar" for me inch-by-inch, keeping me motivated every time I wanted to get comfortable (or, rather, lazy – childishly complaining that I had too much to do).

My sister said, "You're strong. More than you know." She said this at age eighteen, still nearly a child herself, when she gave me courage on the day I (a ten-year-old) was told that our father had died.

My niece, Mihaela, said right after I started my own business, "No one can do it better than you."

When my husband listened to my worries about how my business would work out, he said, "Just look at the name of your company – Optimist Writer – and move ahead." My husband and my children cheer me daily with their hugs and presence in my life.

There are also friends and strangers who cheer and support me.

Yes, strangers help me too. At least, they were strangers when I first met them, mere moments before they gave me gifts of encouragement and support.

For example, during the six years that my husband and I tried to become parents, people who heard what we were going through showed compassion and understanding – doctors, nurses, other couples trying to create a family, or families with children.

There was the time when I was worried about something I don't remember now, and a stranger on a train started a pleasant chat which brightened my day.

There was the beautiful stranger dressed in a red sari who smiled at me at the Copenhagen airport. Right afterwards, I felt the frown that had been straining my forehead a moment before, disappear. As if someone had ironed it away. Her smile, and the uplifting feeling it gave me, accompanied me the whole day after that and still comes to my mind often today.

There were strangers, too, who became the dearest of friends.

References in this chapter:

* http://bit.ly/2tjYYVK

Introduction (Part 2) –

The Story Behind This Project

This project of cheerleading for writers is a gift I am passing along. I first received it from Marcy, Marcella Belson, who lives an ocean and a continent away from me, and whom – as I write this – I still haven't met in person yet.

Marcy found me through my blog. She commented on the very first short story that I edited and published in one piece. Today, this story is available as a free e-book on my website, in a further revised and improved version entitled, "Between Grace and Abyss."

I answered Marcy's comment. And she replied.

Here is our first exchange, which I am glad I saved as a separate file. After migrating the blog from one host to another, many of the original comments were lost. But these survived, saved together in a file along with the short story. I was so thrilled that someone I didn't know found my blog and commented. Somehow, even then, I felt that that exchange was something extraordinary. How right I was!

Marcy, April 23, 2013, 2:37 am:

"Nice going, you have the touch! I enjoyed the story and also, your comments about your own life and child. I'm envious of your ability to write fiction. Looking forward to the next story! Where are you? I'm on the West coast, and it appears you are posting in the middle of the night. Maybe you are!"

I was so excited to read this. Someone thought that my fiction was great and was even envious of my ability to write it! Here is what I answered, a mere ten minutes after Marcy posted her comment.

April 23, 2013, 2:47 am:

"Wow, thank you, Marcy, for the great feedback! I was a bit nervous about this one. Its first version definitely needed thorough editing, but I didn't want to change the story by doing it. So, it was a very interesting challenge.

I live in Denmark, and I write after my day work (working mostly from home) and after spending time with my family. So, I write mostly in the evenings and nights. It is just so much fun to write and share! And read, of course! I am crazy about reading!

Thank you very much again for reading and your feedback!"

Less than two hours later Marcy replied to my comment.

Marcy, April 23, 2013, 4:19 am:

"Oh, Vichizli, thank you for replying to my comment! I'm so happy to have a writer in Denmark that I can

follow your work! I have had several Danish friends over the years, but have never visited Denmark, unfortunately. I write little things for The Elder Storytelling Place, about my life, and I belong to a writers' group. I'll be waiting for your next work!"*

I couldn't wait until the evening to answer to Marcy. So, with a cup of espresso next to my computer, I replied to her during a short break from my work.

April 23, 2013, 9.27 am:

"Dear Marcy, I am really glad to interact with you. I'm a freshman in writing and happy to exchange with people who are as passionate about writing as I am. I just read your story "Bicycles and Glass Bottles" in the Elder Storytelling Place, which surprised me pleasantly with the richness of details. On the first sight, you could say it contains just facts, but hidden emotions were coming through. I won't be able to post there ;), being ten years younger than the admittance age, but I would like to read the stories shared there. I enjoyed yours very much. …"

My comment continued, and I told her a little about Denmark, how I like living here. I was so eager to share more, so I told her that I was originally from Moldova and that I had also lived in Germany. And I recommended all three countries for visiting.

Marcy commented on most of the subsequent posts.

At some point, I realized that our conversations became more personal and more private.

Marcy didn't have my email address then, but I had hers through her subscription to my blog. So I decided to reach out and sent her an email.

From there, our beautiful friendship became stronger every day. I haven't met her in person yet, but it is as if we have known each other for years.

We shared pictures of ourselves and our loved ones. Then little gifts followed. Marcy took photos holding or wearing the gifts I sent her (including a shawl my mother knitted for her). I reported to her how my son didn't want to wear any other socks except the ones Marcy had sent him.

We wrote to each other about writing, about books we'd read, about life, about memories. A generation, an ocean, and a continent, as well as different cultures and upbringing didn't separate us. In fact, they brought us closer together because we were so curious about each other.

Marcy witnessed my writing when I thought I would never want to write a book, when I was certain that I'd stick with sharing short pieces on my blog only.

At some point, I told her about a piece of advice I'd read somewhere: "If there is something you are scared of or worry about, then write about it." (You will find the exact quote in Chapter "B - Book.") I told her there was a story I couldn't stop thinking about. My father's story. How he lost his family during World War II and then attempted to find it.

I admitted to Marcy that I had started writing the book about my father.

In the same email, I told Marcy that I'd been reading a lot about the craft of writing and how most experienced writers advised not to give a first draft to anyone else to read until it was finished and had been revised into at least a second draft.

Marcy said she hoped to be able to read it when it was ready. She then wrote that her doctors suspected cancer and she was awaiting the results.

Having received so much support from such a dedicated reader, I wanted to give back. So I took everything I'd written of first book up to that point, self-edited it and sent it to her with a warning that it was still very raw material.

Fortunately, Marcy's diagnosis was not cancer. But the reminder of the fragility of life – my father and many relatives died of cancer when I was growing up – made me want to tell her the whole story as soon as I could.

Her response to the first chapters was prompt. Marcy had loved what I sent her and couldn't wait for more. She asked me about the Soviet Union and for more details about my father's story. She seemed to be as engaged in the story as I was.

So, I sent her each chapter as soon as it was written and self-edited. I tried to answer each of Marcy's emails quickly and sent her new pages with almost every reply. That got the book going.

Marcy didn't set any deadlines and didn't tell me "you have to write." When it took me time to answer, she always showed compassion for my schedule, which included a full-time job, family responsibilities and volunteer work.

What motivated me most was her unique feedback to each chapter. She told me what moved her and what memories of her own youth and childhood the various scenes of my story reminded her of. From Marcy, I learned the word *cliffhangers* and was delighted when she "accused" me of mastering them.

Our exchange of blog comments and emails continues to this day. Some time ago, we started to talk on the phone about once a month. It is wonderful to hear each other's voices. I wish (naively, I know, but still) that this exchange will never end, and I hope to meet this sweet cheerleader of my writing in person someday. She cannot travel long distances anymore, so I am determined to earn as much as possible from my writing so that I can afford to travel half the globe to meet her. And to hug her.

I would like to finish this chapter with one of the many encouraging comments I received from Marcy, and which shows the power of her cheerleading. I hope that it reveals why I treasure Marcy's support so much:

"I'll be waiting, Vica! Can't imagine how this will evolve...but I have faith in your abilities."

References in this chapter:

* http://www.timegoesby.net/elderstorytelling/marcy-belson/

Introduction (Part 3) –

What This Book is...and

is Not About

What the book is *not* about

It is not meant to support your ego.

If you have ever written more than a page for someone else (a friend, a future employer, an agent or a publisher) to read, then you would know how your ego behaves.

The ego is something that judges you, claims that what you write is not good enough, that you're not cut out to be an author.

It's that distant critic who says without looking, "I already know. It's all bad."

It can also trick you into believing that it is your creative self by saying, "This part wasn't too bad. Now, write the rest in the exact same way."

No, this book is not meant for that part of you. But neither is it intended to judge that part of you. Each part has a reason to be there. Without it, you wouldn't be you.

What the book *is* about

This book is to support your "creative genius." That is how Elizabeth Gilbert, the best-selling author of "Eat, Pray, Love" describes it in her first TED talk* – this mysterious force that makes us create things we never expected to produce but are immensely glad we did.

This book is also meant to support your heart, which blooms when you witness a sunset, which seems to stop beating when you smell a beautiful flower, or breathe in the air rising from the damp soil after a rain shower.

It's the part of you who knows deep inside that there is not one, but an infinite number of perfect ways to do the same thing. That even in a moment of creativity, there is always more than one ideal solution. And that all of them are perfect. Not loved by all in the world, but perfect on their own. That when you grab one by the hand and keep going, it will lead you to completely unexpected adventures inside your imagination and your perception of the world.

This book is meant to cheer the part of you which is able to wonder, to say "Wow!", to draw a big gulp of fresh air and pause to feel how it warms up inside you.

Yes, if you pause and look closer, you will notice that inside of what you've written, among all those words you'd like to rip apart, to strike through with your red pen until it pinches through the page, among those dead leaves you will find a pearl, and then another.

No, I am not referring here to your "darlings" either. Those seemingly beautiful words and phrases which you defend, but others stumble over (and if you are honest with yourself, you do too), the ones that draw all the attention to themselves and don't allow the story, its text, to flow.

No, I am referring to something else. I am talking about the pearls which have universes inside – moving, flowing, dashing universes that sweep you so easily away. Those pearls that magnetically draw you to look inside them and make you forget yourself.

If you love writing, then you can recognize these pearls in the works by others. Reading them is likely what nudged you to write in the first place, the wish to create this kind of magic on your own.

You might not believe me now, but you can create those perfect pearls. And you most probably have already. If not on paper or on a computer screen, then in your imagination in a story you told a friend, whose face brightened when you said it out loud.

References in this chapter:

* https://www.ted.com/talks/elizabeth_gilbert_on_genius

Introduction (Part 4) –

Why I Wrote This Book and

How to Use It

Why I wrote this book

My cheerleaders helped me. Even today, they encourage me to recognize those brilliant pearls inside my writing and creations. I would like to help you find and identify those pearls inside your creations too.

I will not be able to guide you from the first to last chapter of your first or next book, as my dear friend Marcy did for me. But I can guide you through different aspects of writing, creativity, and life...in alphabetical order.

I will guide you from A to Z. One word (sometimes more), one letter, at a time.

How to use this book

As with any book, it is ultimately up to you how to use it. You can read it at your own pace and in the order you like. You can answer or discuss with your fellow writers the questions at the end of (almost) each chapter of this book, or you can move on without concrete answers and jump to another section.

A word of caution, though. Do not inspect or judge your writing by comparing it to what I mention about my own creative process and writing. Such an approach will not motivate you. Rather, it will depress you, whatever your comparison might be.

My suggestion is that you read a chapter, and simply smile if it makes you smile. Smile if you realize how powerful your imagination and creativity are. Smile when you observe the quirky ways in which your mind works. And then forget all about it. These epiphanies are tools. And they are yours forever. They will appear when you need them most. So just relax, let your creative genius take you by the hand, and let the magic begin!

A – Action

And…action!

When it comes to this topic, my mind plays many tricks on me. It often leaps into action and starts generating ideas long before or long after I have at least some of the necessary equipment required for creative writing to take place. For example, many ideas come when I am taking a shower or just about to put my head on my pillow to sleep.

Then, when I am in the process of writing, it often takes another turn and doesn't follow the "brilliant" thoughts I had before. That disappoints my brain. I deliberately say it is my brain which is disappointed and not me, because inevitably when I look back at what I have written, I find many pieces that are even better than the initial ideas.

Finally, when I've finished writing for the day, or morning or afternoon, thoughts appear which are various versions of the following, "There's no action, no fire in your writing!"

These thoughts also appear when I am in the process of writing, urging me to stress myself with endless improving and improving.

They appear around my already published work too.

My first book, *The Truth About Family*, is unique to me. It is rooted in a true story of my father's life, and I find this story exciting and gripping.

But my thoughts behave like a person who wants to diminish the merit of this work and say, "Somebody will believe that it's boring."

My answer to these thoughts are, "Of course there will be someone who won't like the book and will find it annoying. Probably because this person has different interests. But do I write for this person? No. I write for those who might be moved by this story as it moved me."

The interesting thing is that these negative thoughts do not appear when I open the book and read a passage, remembering both my father and so many inspiring moments during the creation of the book.

These thoughts appear when I am already complaining and don't realize it. When that happens, any uplifting and constructive thought is dismissed with an annoyed hand-wave.

What helps is to let myself observe all of my internal and external reactions, without labelling them as good or bad. Only then I can find the fun during the authoring process and enjoy the results of my writing.

I've discovered that when I reread something from my published books, I can't stop reading it until I finish a passage or a chapter. There is this novelty, this curiosity. *Did I write this?*

It is also fun to realize that every time I read one of my published pieces, I am a different person with at least slightly divergent views and inclinations. I can continually experience my books and articles anew, and I can experience the world around me — including my creations — anew as well.

These days, I experience more and more frequent moments of kindness toward myself. What helped me reach this point? Two things.

The first is practicing awareness and being fully present in the moment of now. This simple but brilliant approach of Instantaneous Transformation, which I mentioned in the preface and which was developed by award-winning authors Ariel and Shya Kane, is a fair, kind and honest companion that helps me to realize that my thoughts are not me. These thoughts were formed when I was a child, first learning how to speak. They were shaped throughout my life, as I continued learning and interacting with the ever-changing world around me. Now, I have the choice to listen to them or let them be, whether they bring a creative idea or a nervous one dreading the unknown.

The second great helper for me is the feedback of my friends and fans.

There must be something about your writing when your readers and friends say or write something like this:

"I read this book from beginning to end the day I received it. It was captivating! An easy to read book and one of the best books I have read all year."

or

"This is a very well written story about finding your identity and yourself in the young years, and I was drawn into the author's universe from page one. It is one of those books you don't want to finish because you have come to care for the persons and their stories."

Both reviews above were written about *The Truth About Family*, the book that my brain feared would be labelled as boring.

If you have doubts about your writing, observe yourself, the room around you, everything in the given moment of now, and then look closer.

Yes, look closer, and I am sure you will find scenes in your manuscript, that you wish to continue, that you don't want to end.

Action is in your nature. It keeps you alive. There is also action in your writing. Just hold onto the feeling of excitement you get when you read a captivating book. Observe yourself without judging what you see, and more and more often you'll experience those same moments of excitement while writing, and later reading, the pieces you've written.

P.S.

Though, as I write this postscript, I have written and published nine books since *The Truth About Family*, I still occasionally have the concern that I wouldn't be able to offer enough action in my stories. In 2016, I submitted my second fiction book, *A Spy's Daughter*, to the 24th Annual Writer's Digest Self-Published Book Awards. Here is the review I received from one of their judges:

"I'm a big fan of spy fiction, and, until recently, it has been rare to see a strong female protagonist; John le Carré's Charlie in THE LITTLE DRUMMER GIRL is one of the earliest to come to mind. The thing I like most about Victoria Ichizli-Bartels's A SPY'S DAUGHTER is that an interesting woman is at the center of the story. It's European setting and post-Soviet mood are also incredibly appealing. Ichizli-Bartels does a good job of scene setting and character development. My main issue with the book seems to be with its pacing. The novel moves a little bit too swiftly for my taste, and it seems as though just when we're getting into a chapter and settling in, the scene is cut off. Perhaps I'm a bit too used to the kind of spy fiction that le Carré writes, which is slowly and deliberately paced. The pacing here often feels perhaps a bit more suited to the screen than to the page—this would make an excellent screenplay. But since this is also book one in a series, perhaps this issue would seem less noticeable when all of the books are read together. Having said that, the book's plot is fascinating, and the protagonist extremely well-drawn, which isn't always the case with spy fiction."

It seems that the only deficiency of the book was too much action. *Hm.* Yet another proof that fears, especially in a creative world, are a waste of time.

B – Book

Back in 2013, I looked at my wishes and discovered I had a big dream – looming and raising its head above water for some time but previously pushed aside and hidden – to write and share my writing. At the same time, I had the idea that I didn't want to write a book. I didn't consider a short story (which I had gathered some practice at writing by then) to be a book, and writing a novel appeared daunting and time-consuming. I thought I couldn't be as patient as other authors and wait that long until my books were published.

I wanted to share immediately after creating something. Starting a blog was the solution.

Around this time, I read a German translation of the book *Writing Down the Bones: Freeing the Writer Within* by Natalie Goldberg and found there the following words:

"Write what disturbs you, what you fear, what you have not been willing to speak about. Be willing to be split open."*

There was one story that surfaced again and again. At first, I thought it was my sad story of having lost my father when I was ten years old. I felt sorry for myself for not being able to talk to him as an adult. I judged others when I saw them arguing with their fathers. I regretted that I didn't know him in my teen years, that he didn't see me grow up and follow the various paths of my life, that I wasn't able to argue with him, to laugh with him, to ask for advice.

Tasting the experience of Instantaneous Transformation and becoming aware of my tricky thought processes changed everything. I saw that I was victimizing myself and avoiding something. Then I realized what that something was.

I was avoiding my father's story. His story of losing his family during World War II and trying to find them. Of finding them, only to be met with disappointment and rejection. I thought his story was an unfortunate one.

So I pushed it away. But it kept coming back. In hindsight, I understand that it was natural for it to come back. This story is a part of my family heritage. It is a part of me.

But back then I resisted it and resisted some more. It kept returning in my thoughts, and I grew tired of this internal fight. I needed to address it.

Natalie Goldberg's words came to my aid and this idea that *maybe I should write about it* started appearing and re-appearing, intriguing me with exponentially growing intensity.

It all happened very fast because hardly a few months after launching my blog, I started writing a novel about my dad.

As soon as I began, the process ran almost seamlessly. I experimented with voices, with characters, stories, settings, whole chapters, grew frustrated about some of them. But the question about to write or not to write a book disappeared. I was simply too deep inside the whole adventure to worry about it.

It wasn't until I was over half way through the book and fairly close to the end that I again started fearing to work on this book and this story. But it was already too late. Quite a few people knew about it and liked it. Quitting was not an option. Not to mention that explaining the reasons for giving up would take much more effort than simply finishing the novel. The story itself and the way I wrote it was at least partially responsible for cementing those people who had read it as my cheerleaders. The conclusion was simple: I couldn't disappoint them. I had to finish it.

And so I did. I finished it, revised it, revised some more, let others read it, revised again, had it edited and read again. And then one night in 2015, almost two years after I started writing this story down, I published it. My first book was born.

And another was already on the way. I was eager to write and create more books. I tasted the joy and magic of creating, and I witnessed what effect my creations had on others. They ignited something very personal. I saw people smile and heard from my mother how pleasantly surprised our relatives in Moldova were when they found out about my first book. She told me about the hugs they gave her and the memories they shared with her about my father.

The brief fear that my first novel would be a 'one-time wonder' disappeared as soon as I published my second book the same year, shortly before Christmas.

Then a short story came out a little while later. As a book of its own. Right after that I started to blog several books in parallel and finished them one after another. The lines you read right now belong to yet another book. More are appearing on other days, and still more will be born.

Yes, the person who writes these lines was sure she would never write a book, and even that she didn't want to write one. The truth I discovered was that I not only wanted to write books but also that I needed to create something every day.

Writing my first book also closed many wounds I thought were open. I found that my father's story was a beautiful story, with some sad moments but also joyful ones, and all of them deep and special.

After this experience, I am sure that any person – if he or she wants it – can write a book or create something else equally unique. All we have to own is a wish to do it, a will to pursue and a passion to help us carry our work successfully towards completion.

I discovered that I had all three. It was an amazing discovery. And with every new project, I find this again and again.

You might think, "It's all well and good for you. But I won't be able to write a book. I was thinking about it. But I have so much on my plate. It is simply not possible. I will never manage it."

If you think any of these, then please consider the following:

If you gather all the emails, all the posts on social media you have written, you might discover that have you authored an encyclopaedia.

You might argue that this is not creative and that it was not for a higher purpose.

Are you sure? Was there, among your emails or posts, one directed to uplift or support a friend or family member? I bet there was. And I bet more than one! I also bet that if you read them, you would discover beautiful metaphors, analogies, and stories you have shared.

Of course, you and I might argue for hours, you wanting to prove that you can't write, and me trying to show you the opposite.

And we will both be right because there are moments when we stay stuck in our ways, and also moments when we let ourselves be creative.

And we might both be wrong, right? From the point of view of the other.

So let's just sit in the chair of the other and consider how this changes our points of view.

If I sit in your chair, I look around, draw a deep breath and see. Yes, I am familiar with this outlook. Even now, after having done a Ph.D. thesis and published ten books, I still have moments where I think, I can't write books. Especially likable ones. The kind of books that are bought and read and ignite the reader's wish to have more words from my pen. My thoughts also try to convince me that those books I have written and published were a case of pure luck, of some unknown force pushing me through. These thoughts try to make me believe that I have no power of my own to accomplish this. Yes, I still have these thoughts and they pop up during my writing and ask for my attention.

Now, what if you sat in my optimistic chair? Can you see that you can do it?

I think, here, some good old clichés are called for. Everyone has a book in them. And if you set up your mind to it, you can write one. And much more after that. If I could do it, you can too.

C – Characters

Characters are multi-dimensional, especially the ones reader's love. To me, the notion of creating a character has many dimensions too. Here is my story about creating characters and my discoveries along the way.

Writers and the characters they create

There are excellent resources on how to build great characters. There are books and articles. There are unforgettable characters in literature to tap and learn from.

All this enchants me. But also scares me. And even terrifies me at times.

I should learn more. I should learn more. The thought used to appear in my head from time to time, and sometimes still does, whirling like a tornado.

Ever since I heard "It's all about characters" and "If the reader can't sympathize with your character, then your book is doomed," I've been scared that the characters I create are not good enough. And since I saw my reflection in them, then I wasn't good enough either.

Things that happen when writers dive into the world of their characters

So, I began going through checklists of what makes a great character, scrutinizing and criticizing my characters. But there were also gaps in time when I forgot my worries and forgot those warnings. I just wrote and lived inside my characters' world. I wondered about them, I argued with them. Some of them started arguing with me in my head. All by themselves. Sometimes I had to challenge particular characters before they would show their nature to me. Some became my friends. Like friends you no longer have contact with but are happy to have had them in your life. Friends who've shared memories that you cherish. Friends you've met by surprise or on purpose.

Some of my characters brought people to life who are long gone.

To write about my father was one of the biggest gifts I gave myself. To write about a time in his life that I never had a chance to witness was unexpectedly rewarding.

An amazing thing happened when I started writing *The Truth About Family* from the first person. It was a strange thing to do, as I had begun writing my dad's story in the third person. But changing the point of view to the first person brought him to life. His younger self started, in a way, talking to me. Sometimes I felt as if he was dictating the words. My father became my friend, just as

I'd always wanted and thought was impossible since I was only ten years old when he died.

But even purely fictional characters in my books – reflections of people I love, meet and cherish in my life, as well as myself – became friends, and their destiny became important to me.

As I started observing myself in the process of writing and especially in the process of self-editing, a few curious things happened. And with them came a few important realizations.

Characters are real

I was reading a chapter from my book *A Spy's Daughter* in which my protagonist Hannah tells something about her past to another character, and I caught myself thinking, *Oh, this happened to me too!* I had to laugh. Of course, it did! *I* wrote that.

I have a friend whom I met at a conference in Budapest in 2008 and have held dear ever since. Her name is Corinne Rockweiler, or simply Corky. When I was preparing *A Spy's Daughter* for publication, Corky sent me a memoir written by her father. In it, he talked fondly about his wife who, before their marriage, worked for the CIA.

Right after receiving this, I wrote the following to Corky in an email, which I titled "Coincidences and other wonderful matters":

"Wow, your mother worked for the CIA! I exclaim because of two reasons. Well, not every day someone works for the CIA. And the second reason is that the mother of the protagonist in my second book also worked for the CIA. :)"

After hitting "send," I realized that my protagonist was a fictional character and that the facts about her were not quite real. So I wrote to Corky:

"It's funny how I talk about my characters as if they were real people. ;)"

Corky's response was utterly motivating and uplifting:

"I often get attached to characters in a book! No reason you shouldn't see them as real people since you 'gave birth' to them :)"

This message lit a bright lightbulb inside me. My characters are real because I am real!

A little later I re-discovered in my collection of stationery a notebook with the following quote from Pablo Picasso on its cover,

"Everything you can imagine is real."

Why a writer frowns during self-edit

One day during a self-edit, I found myself frowning. That particular moment that I noticed my frown was revealing and surprising for me. I love referring to this discovery often.

As I considered my frown, I realized that it wasn't a reaction to the loud voice in my head judging my writing as awful, which happens every so often. I realized that I had frowned because Hannah, the protagonist in *A Spy's Daughter*, was frowning too. She was in a desperate situation at that point in her story and I truly felt for her.

After this observation, and the smile that came with it, I returned to my writing, adding a few intensifying touches to the scene that made it sharper and more vivid.

Observe yourself without judging

You have already heard me suggest this many times, and you will hear me say it again and again.

Observe yourself when you read your writing. And do this without judging yourself.

Then you might discover that, although you didn't explicitly describe some of the character traits of your protagonist or antagonist, you still see and feel them. And in the next moment, you understand that they will be just as visible for your readers. Though the readers will no doubt add eye color, shades, and other features, according to their preferences, they will still get a clear picture of who these characters are.

Your characters are real because you are real.

D – Descriptions

I used to think all descriptions longer than one line were annoying. In the books I read, I wanted to skip them, while at the same time making myself read them and victimizing myself that I had to do this. In writing, I tried to skip them too. And more than that, an idea formed in my mind, *I am not able to write descriptions.*

Then two things happened. The first one had to do with reading descriptions.

Reading descriptions

Here is what I wrote in July 2014 in a blog post called "A Discovery about Descriptions".*

One of the things I used to dislike in books were long descriptions. Even descriptions by such masters as Leo Tolstoy and Jane Austen made me sometimes quite impatient, and my brain was thinking, *When will the story continue?*

I was sure this was a result of my impatience, not the lack of virtue of the pieces I read. But still, these experiences made me afraid to create my own descriptions when I started writing fiction myself.

And then several months before writing this blog post, I read *The Signature of All Things* by Elizabeth Gilbert and became completely dumbfounded. The book was amazing and…full of descriptions! Many of them pages and pages long. How could that be?

I found the answer in an article in Writer's Digest from January 2014 by Elizabeth Sims, which I read not long afterwards. The title of the article was "Miscalculations and Missteps."** And there, in Section 6 – "The Great Undescribed," I found the following:

"Take a risk and go long. *The value of a relatively long description is that it draws your readers deeper into the scene. The worry is that you'll bore them. But if you do a good job you'll engross them. Really getting into a description is one of the most fun things you can do as an author. Here's the trick: Get going on a description with the attitude of* **discovering,** *not* **informing.** *In this zone, you're not writing to tell readers stuff you already know – rather, you are writing to discover and experience the scene right alongside them."*

This passage revealed to me the secret of the SOAT (as Elizabeth Gilbert calls *The Signature of All Things),* which was unclear for me before that. The SOAT is full of descriptions, but each description is full of discoveries: of love, of one's own body, of lust, of science, of mother nature, of the secrets of the universe and its origins, and much more. The whole book is a continuous discovery. You can hear this wonder in the voice of the narrator, who mirrors the wonder of the main character, Alma Whittaker, as she experiences it throughout her journey.

The book also covers a time period of more than 50 years! That again goes against the advice I learned, "The shorter the timeframe, the better. Backstory can go further back, but the plot itself should unfold in a short period. Otherwise, you will bore the reader."

But the SOAT proves this advice completely wrong. It starts with Alma's birth and finishes with her death. This story covering a whole life of its protagonist and beyond fascinated millions of readers and became an international bestseller.

Even at her death, Alma is still discovering. One reader's review of the SOAT describes Alma as *"insatiably curious."* And I became more and more curious with every sentence I read of Alma's story.

I am very grateful to both Elizabeths (Gilbert and Sims) for lifting my fear of descriptions, for showing me that I can love reading long descriptions and wish for more, and for giving me a great clue for how to recognize an excellent one.

All this led me to a thought which applies to everything:

One of the clues to having fun, along with being in the moment, is to be in a constant mode of discovery, walking through life 'with an open mouth' and being in awe of everything inside and around ourselves.

Writing descriptions

Fast forward one year later, when I first wrote this chapter that you are reading now. By this time, I was sure there were brilliant descriptions that could captivate me. So I started approaching each book I read and wrote with curiosity about both dialogue and descriptions. But there was still a problem. I didn't believe I was capable of writing good descriptions, not to mention captivating ones.

Then one evening I went to a meeting of the writers' club I attend here in Aalborg, Denmark. I hadn't managed to write something completely new for that particular evening, so I took with me the first chapter of a story I had recently posted online .

This story, which eventually became a novelette, is called *Nothing Is As It Seems*. And it came to life after I watched a "one-minute writing class" video created by my writing teacher and friend Menna van Praag. As an exercise to develop a story, she had suggested we start with the first paragraph of her best-selling book *The House at the End of Hope Street*,*** and then continue writing and creating our own story from there.

So, at the writers' club meeting, I sat in a comfortable armchair in the cozy living room atmosphere of two of our writing club members and read out loud to them this first chapter of my new story. As I read it, I realized, *The chapter is full of descriptions. And they are good!*

When I finished reading, I looked up with the still-unprocessed shock of this discovery on my face. *I can write good descriptions?!*

The feedback from my fellow writers added to the shock. They liked the chapter too. The only correction they offered was about the way I pronounced the word *wrapped*. My thoughts went wild. *Really? Only this? And the rest is all good?*

After that, they pointed out the especially good parts of the piece. I had to agree. They were good, and I liked reading them aloud.

Of course, there were still bits to be tweaked here and there, and I did so before sending the whole story to my editor. And the story did become much better after the edits. But on that evening, I understood that this piece was something I wouldn't be ashamed to read out loud again.

Thus, my advice here to you, dear writer, whether you have problems with descriptions or not, watch out for those labels you give yourself, your writing, your reading abilities, and anything you do. Observe them, lift their edges and peek underneath. You might discover that those labels are long outdated, and might not have been true all along.

At this point, I would like to tell you one of my favorite jokes: a man was asked whether he could play a violin. His answer was, "I don't know. I never tried!"

So, let's approach everything with this attitude. Let's not say, "I can't do something," until we try, and try again. We might discover that we can, are very good at it, and that we even enjoy doing what we want or have to do.

References in this chapter:

* http://victoriaichizlibartels.com/a-discovery-about-descriptions/

** http://www.writersdigestshop.com/writers-yearbook-2014

*** http://www.mennavanpraag.com/books/

E – Editing

We, authors, want our creations to be read and loved. And most of us would agree that before the readers get to see any written word, it needs to be scanned and checked by one or more pairs of eyes. Other than ours.

Many of us have learned from brilliant writing teachers and great books that we need to trust our editors, that if they have a strong opinion about something, it is likely that our readers will have issues with those same bits too.

But when the moment comes to send our stories to editors or beta-readers – friends or other friendly readers willing to "taste" our stories before (or after) they are professionally edited – we get cold feet. We even might revise our work tens of times because we think that it is not ready or not good enough to be seen by somebody else.

Here are a couple of fearful thoughts (and the stories connected to them) that my brain used to generate before I sent my work to somebody else to read.

"They won't like my story!"

I sent a revised draft of *A Spy's Daughter* to three beta-readers. Two have answered and gave feedback. They loved it. One of them, my niece Mihaela, edited the book thoroughly, and her input turned out to be a great line edit. Mihaela didn't have any major objections or changes to suggest.

The third reader, my friend (and editor of the book you read now) Leah Schneeflock, and I agreed on a later deadline for her feedback because of the commitments she had. As we emailed about this deadline, she wrote that she loved what she read so far.

And still, my brain kept creating scenarios in which Leah's final feedback would contain harsh words of criticism claiming that it was the worst book she'd ever read. Even re-reading her initial feedback didn't help. Those thoughts of unworthiness of my creations kept coming back.

I did hope for positive feedback from Leah, and sometimes I tried to fantasize what she might say, but at the end, the pessimistic thoughts prevailed. What came from her, in reality, was completely unexpected. Along with constructive, insightful and brilliant ideas for how to improve various parts of my book, Leah wrote the following:

"What a great story! And there were so many beautiful poetic lines of writing. Here are a couple of my faves. (I only jotted down a few, there were many more...)

- *'So different from the gray day outside. And all so different from her gray life outside of this building.'*

- *'Liam's hands searched for non-existing side-pockets in his boxer-shorts.'*

- *'Hannah nodded in answer to him and managed to smuggle a few words into the conversation.'"*

Leah's feedback startled me, but at the same time was reassuring and encouraging.

The next step was to revise and send the book to my editor in the US, Rob Bignell.

And the same scenario repeated itself. Midway through reading, Rob wrote that he very much liked the book. Yet my automatic thoughts reappeared declaring that his final words would be a guillotine for my story.

They weren't. Rob pointed out a few consistent issues that I could learn from (I have since added his suggestion to my self-editing checklist) and made line edits for the rest.

What helped was to notice how automatically these self-judging thoughts appeared and that they were like recordings, repetitious and unchanging. Fortunately, seeing this without criticizing myself, and being curious about my readers and editors feedback was, in the end, stronger than fear. Curiosity prevailed, as well as the newfound and highly-appreciated will to be both kind and honest to myself.

But my brain is very creative in generating new (or rather seemingly new) worries.

"I'm not able to remember everything my editors taught me! Therefore, I will never be a great writer!"

My next worry was that my editors and beta-readers would always point out the same mistakes and tell me that I am not able to learn. I was afraid that I wouldn't be able to remember all the realizations and lessons gained from their edits and comments, and that I would make the same mistakes again and again.

I am lucky to have a terrific friend who pops up to help many times every day. This friend is awareness. Granting her – I like thinking of awareness as one of my very best girlfriends – time and attention brings plenty of awards. In the above scenario, she shrugged and said,

"So what!? Of course you will forget some of the lessons learned, and of course you will remake some of the mistakes. But there will also be many that you won't repeat, and many of those you seem to repeat will have a new context. The mistakes are not mistakes. They are just adjustments on your way. So simply have fun with what you are experiencing."

Hm, I thought. *She might be right.*

So I tried something out when I was going through the edits of my very first book *The Truth About Family* (later also with subsequent books). I went through all of the specific comments by my brilliant editor and cover designer Alice Jago and addressed them, adjusting the text to resolve any issues she pointed out. After that, I accepted all the changes without looking at any of them in detail, moved the manuscript to a new file, printed everything out, and let it rest for a few days.

Then, as mentioned above, I read the manuscript without checking each of the edits from Alice. I decided to treat the new version of the book as our team effort and read it as such. I loved what I read and noticed myself doing, by hand, three types of comments and markings:

- Bits I stumbled upon, or items which needed to be addressed and modified (whether they were simply typing errors or larger inconsistencies).

- Pieces I liked and was excited about. I wanted to see who came up with each great idea – Alice, my editor, or me.

- Words that were new to me and which appeared in the edits, or the words I knew but was unfamiliar with in a specific context. These related directly to the first bullet above.

Then I tracked those (and only those) bits inside the file where all of the change suggestions were still marked. What I discovered there – and what has happened to me every time I worked with an editor since then – was both humbling and uplifting.

There were changes that my editors suggested but upon which I stumbled. These I changed back or modified in an entirely different way (the latter happened in most cases). When I fixed those bits, I felt best when not criticizing either side, but just recognizing that there was a misunderstanding, that an action was needed, and that I am ultimately the one responsible for the quality and outcome of my books. Then I stumbled upon bits that were untouched by the editor but asked for changes. I saw that there was more room to improve my writing.

Now to the great bits. These were the ones that made me both humble and proud. Humble because I saw how much better my writing became due to the contribution of my editors and beta-readers – how they added color, crispness and greatness – and because I realized that they cared about my writing and about me as a writer and a person. I also felt a sense of pride because I discovered that some of the most beautiful parts (often surprisingly to me) were my own original writing. These great bits, being mine all along, were also humbling because my ego realized that all the daydreaming and plans and vain discussions inside my head were not responsible for all those great bits. These were the moments of creativity, the amazing moments of now, the ones where I let my true self come to its full expression that my ego and the rest of me have to thank.

I hope that my tales above inspire you to observe yourself without judging – how your ego and thoughts are often harsh toward yourself, and how they try to preoccupy you when there is something scary, new, or even exciting to do, something pulling you out of your comfort zone. Observe the tone of your beta-readers, your editors, and the tone of your thoughts. Refer only to the comments of the kind editors and beta-readers. Those who are unkind are at least as harsh to themselves as you are to yourself, probably even more so.

Welcome the edits, thank those who proposed them, and, again, look at all this as a big, fun game.

It is a game, and the more you practice it, the better you will become.

So, let's practice. I'll do it along with you.

F – Frankfurt Book Fair

(or a Tale about Illusions)

I'm talking a lot about my brain (and human brains, in general) in this book, and how observing its worrying and survival-oriented nature – as well as not judging it – helps me stop complaining and instead pursue what I want to do, namely, writing.

I have also mentioned how creative it is – this wonderful invention of nature that lives inside my head. Creative, when producing new worries.

But of course, it is also creative in constructive ways – during the generation and realization of new ideas. During the actual creative process, which lets me grow spiritually and bloom physically.

And there's another way my brain can be creative. By creating dreams – rational, constructive ones that motivate me to be curious and passionate about what I am doing.

And then, there are illusions.

The Frankfurt Book Fair and later, due to the geographic proximity and budget required to participate, The

Gothenburg Book Fair, were in my fantasies when I was writing my first book.

Here is what happened.

Big book events fascinated me. I had never attended one. I still haven't, even now.

I did attend some other big fairs. The Hanover Fair, for example, where I manned one of the booths of the Technical University Darmstadt in the late 1990s. There, I had a taste of what it means to be an exhibitor and also the opportunity to go around and network as a visitor.

The same happened almost ten years later at the ILA Berlin Air Show (International Aerospace Exhibition and Conferences). I was there with the German branch of the company I worked with at that time. My colleagues and I were thrilled to have visitors at our booth and to gather new leads and create new business relationships for our company.

As an avid reader, I fantasized about The Frankfurt Book Fair and what it would be like to walk among all those shelves of new books, opening them and getting a sneak peek into the newest releases.

As soon as I decided to self-publish my first book, I threw away the fantasies about finding my books in a bookstore, and instead, another fantasy appeared. A fantasy of me sitting at a booth at a book fair with a pile of my books on a table in front of me. People going by, some of them stopping to look curiously at the books before putting them back, and others buying one, then two, then more. There was no end goal in this fantasy, like selling out all of my books, rather to have people be curious about my books and sometimes buy them.

I didn't have any serious intention or plan in place, just a dream. But with the dates for the fairs (both in Frankfurt and Gothenburg) approaching, I started feeling stressed. It became evident that not only would I be unable to publish my book before then – I wouldn't even be able to finish writing its first draft.

OK, I thought. With this being impossible and having been told by a fellow writer that exhibiting books and buying a place at a booth was costly, my brain switched to another fantasy. I had heard about a Self-Publishing Book Award by Writer's Digest* and similar events by Amazon and other organizers. But I got frustrated that I didn't seem able to make those deadlines either.

I started to become aware of my many frustrations, with the help of the Instantaneous Transformation technique developed by Ariel and Shya Kane that I mentioned initially in this book's preface. I started to look at what might be the source of those frustrations. The answer was an idea I had that if I make it to a book fair or win a writing competition, then I will feel better as a writer, then I will feel accomplished.

When I realized this, I was dumbfounded.

Really? Only exhibiting my books at book fairs or winning competitions will define me as an accomplished and satisfied author?

I couldn't believe what my brain was generating because it was simply not true. The facts were completely the opposite.

Here are the facts. Every time I sit down and write I experience accomplishment. Every time I go through the text I have written, I find there something I am not ashamed to share. And every comment, every piece of feedback from a reader shows me that my books, my articles touch them.

Yes, some of my readers don't write to me or comment after reading my books or articles, but this doesn't mean that I have failed as a writer.

Not the amount of feedback, nor the fact that I am not yet earning my full living from my writing are what make me feel like a writer or not. What touches me is that I have found at least one very close friend through my writing alone. And I continue making friends through my writing. The friendship between my friends and me tightens as we read each other's books or enjoy the various outcomes of our creative processes, like music for example. These friendships are absolutely priceless!

Slowing down and becoming aware of all this was and is, every time I realize it, an enormous gift. I am thrilled that I have the possibility to practice and experience this again and again.

The illusionary and self-deprecating thoughts still come from time to time, especially when I go out of my comfort zone and am about to jump into something entirely new and unknown. But with awareness of the real value of writing for me, these thoughts become less and less frequent, and they are not that loud anymore. I realize that these illusions and ideas, which imply that I am not good enough, are just recordings I learned from the cultures I was immersed in along the way, and which were laid stone-by-stone, judgment-by-judgment, by many generations before me – distorted through the lens of my perception.

Today, I realize more and more often that in *every* new moment I have a choice to make. To write and enjoy the creative process or to complain and compare myself to some strange and diffuse version of myself whom I don't even like. And I realize that I am not alone in these discoveries, that more and more people make more and more often the choice to create and be active instead of being afraid, instead of daydreaming illusions. Instead of that, I come back to the process of writing, again and again, enjoying my creativity, including the surprises and emotions it generates in me.

Here are the results of letting go of my fears and turning my attention to creativity instead:

Along with moving houses, working as a consultant and managing a family with two small children and a new business, I published a novel, a novella and a short story within one year, including a full revision and editing process. Beyond that, I wrote and posted two short e-books on my website, published three more books in 2016, finalized several manuscripts, which I am revising now and publishing this year, and have at least three other works-in-progress. (P.S. Two of the three books planned for 2017 were published in Spring of that year and the book you read now is the third published in 2017.) In addition to all of this, I submitted (in 2016 and 2017) two of my books to the Self-Published Book Award at Writer's Digest. Although the first one didn't win, as I mentioned at the end of Chapter "A – Action", and I have not yet received confirmation about the second one, whether they win or not isn't the point of it all. There is something else that matters. I express myself in my writing, and I experience what my books generate in others. And I learn how my motivation and passion for writing infects my fellow writers to do the same.

Yes, all this matters and enriches me.

Dear writer, dear friend, please notice yourself and how your readers react toward your writing. Even the negative feedback shows that your writing has steered your reader. And if you let your heart flow into your writing then I am sure there will be at least one smile on the face of at least one of your readers. *This* is what counts! Nothing else.

There is a funny tendency I have noticed. Negative comments and reviews seem to increase as a writer becomes more popular and gains more readers. Before then, writing produced with heart and quality primarily gets reviewed by those with a vested interest in the writer – this tribe starts with friends and the people he or she deals with on a daily basis, then extends to those who share the writer's interests (and is generally ignored by those who don't). But as the wave of popularity grows, readers who might not enjoy this particular genre are swept along too, and tend to add more critical opinions to the mix.

But if you are like me as I write this article, at the (relative) beginning of a writing and publishing career, then enjoy the support and motivation of your cheerleaders, who enjoy your writing. They might enjoy reading your work as much as you enjoy writing it.

Here is to the true gems we have and can enjoy now in this moment, not to the illusions which fog our vision and veer us away from the brilliant paths we have chosen to walk!

Happy writing and happy creating!

References in this chapter:

* www.writersdigest.com/writers-digest-competitions/self-published-book-awards

G – Genre

There are so many opinions about whether an author should stick with one genre or just follow his or her gut and write whatever comes to mind regardless of known styles, even deliberately trying their hand at a new and unknown genre.

I've read many books and articles urging one or another point of view. All quite convincingly.

Somehow, I listened more to those that said, "Stick with one genre."

I had an idea that I had to write a romantic comedy since I loved reading them. But when I sat down to write, something else came out. Suspense. With some romantic touches. It was more in the genre of women's contemporary literature (especially the series *A Life Upside Down*) with a lot of suspense, family drama and the breath of a thriller.

Not long after, I started telling my friends, "I will never write memoirs. That is simply not me!"

In reply, they shrugged, a bit surprised at my exclamation, as none of them had asked whether I wanted to write a memoir. But I kept repeating it, even when somebody was only asking me what genres I wrote in. Eventually, the ever-returning and threatening statement "But not memoirs!" made me frown. If nobody required me to write one, why did I said *No* aloud?

After some searching and contemplation, I recalled when this idea of "Memoirs-are-not-for-me" formed for the first time. I'd once found a long article about memoirs and eagerly read every word of it. Somewhere in the middle, my thoughts had shouted, "No, this is too complicated. Memoirs are not for me. They are too conflicting and will stir too much worry in me and those I am writing about!"

From that moment, I kept repeating this statement to myself and others, "Memoirs are not for me! I am writing only in one genre!"

The truth, however, was different.

The truth was that my first and second books, which I wrote and published before this strange internal battle about memoirs commenced, were of very different genres. I wasn't writing in one genre to begin with.

My blog posts, on the other hand, had still another unique shape. I avoided thinking about their "shapes" as genres. I still had this idea that I had to and wanted to stick with one style.

But why was I so often thinking of memoirs, when I supposedly write only fiction? Why was I answering this question with a *No*, that no one was even asking? Who was asking me to write a memoir?

As I relaxed, took a step back and looked at it, I had the answer. *I* was the one who wanted to write a memoir. And the fact was that I was already doing it. In my blog, and also in my very first book *The Truth About Family*, which is based on the true story of my father. I wrote this book in the first person as if my dad had written his very own memoir.

As I realized this, I discovered that another genre had snuck into my writing: guide books on business.

How did that happen?

Quite simply, I had recently found a straightforward definition to a seemingly complicated technical subject, one that my colleagues and I had grappled with for many years, and I wanted to share my discovery. So I blogged a book about it, and in the same days that I was writing this chapter, I revised it for publication. (The book was published at the end of March 2017 under the title *Take Control of Your Business: Learn what Business Rules are, discover that you are already using them, then update them to maximize your business success.*)

But writing first fiction and then non-fiction is inconsistent with my aspiration to write in one genre!? What should I do now? I thought that as I detected the multiple styles I had been "messing with."

Awareness and Instantaneous Transformation came to help again. I chose to look non-judgmentally at why I had this idea that I had to write in only one genre. I realized that included in the idea was the assumption that writing in more than one genre would mean delivering writing of bad quality.

I frowned. *Really?* I love reading the works of quite a few authors who write in multiple genres and deliver brilliant and memorable books. Take Elizabeth Gilbert and Stephen King, for example. Both of them write fiction and non-fiction, their non-fiction embracing both the memoir and guide-book styles.

So, why did I choose to listen only to those who said that writers should stick with only one genre? Why did I decide not to hear those who claimed the opposite? Giving these considerations space, slowly I found the answer.

I had taken the recommendation to write in only one genre as an absolute rule, one that I had to follow.

I had completely forgotten that, for these authors, writing in one genre was a personal choice. And that it is utterly human to urge others to do something that works for us. We've all done this at least once in our lives.

But I completely forgot to look at whether their recipe worked for me. When I looked honestly at their recommendation, I found that it didn't work for me. Before considering their advice and my reaction to it non-judgmentally, I had thought I was doing something wrong. But I wasn't. I simply had my own way. And I just needed to look closer to find out what that way was.

As I started investigating these ideas of mine without judging them and seeing the various cultural influences, I discovered something else.

I found the originating idea that had prompted me to listen only to single-genre recommendations. I remembered being told as a child that I could not concentrate for a long period of time on just one thing. I've found out since, that this experience is, in fact, true for many children, if not for all. But at the time, I took it as my personal failure. And I thought for a long time that I was not good at finishing things.

When this old idea appeared again I decided to estimate how much and how little I have finished so far on average.

PhD? Finished.

Work projects? Multiple projects successfully finished.

Books? As of writing this chapter, I have written and published five books (with three for sale at various retailers and two e-books available on my site), plus two more manuscripts are finished and in the pre-editorial draft stage. (As of Summer 2017, having made progress with the self-edit of this book, I have ten books published, with eight in paperback and e-book formats, and two solely in e-book format.)

Personal projects? Multiple successfully planned and facilitated, including a wedding and two christening ceremonies.

And so on.

Unfinished and forgotten? Yes, of course! But nothing prominent. Nothing which I really wanted to be finished. Those that I wanted to get through were seen through. And there are a number of items, which have been started, but are by no means forgotten.

So, there was I with an answer to a riddle that had occupied me for a long time. I had listened to some erroneously understood ideas from long ago, stressed myself by believing them, and judged myself for not being able to follow them.

Another question. Was it worth it? To have lived through this, to have experienced and investigated this dilemma? Yes. Because now I can sigh with relief and tell you about it.

Dear friends, whether it is about writing in various genres or not, I invite you to look at what you say *No* to, particularly when nobody outside yourself has asked you to do this particular something. Look even closer if you say *No* again and again, and repeat it out loud to many clueless listeners. Can it be that this idea you are resisting is actually one of your truest desires? Could the one who suggests this new idea that your brain so eagerly says *No* to, could this maybe be your heart?

H – Hook

(or the Fun-Detecting Antenna)

There were two topics for me as a writer that were almost as daunting and scary as the birth of my first child in 2010.

One was the advice to "Show – don't tell." The other was how to create "hooks" at the beginning of a book or chapter.

I came across many positive examples of hooks in other peoples' writing, but the wrong ones rang the loudest bell and I readily imagined myself able to create only weak hooks. It seemed so easy to start a book badly and so difficult to start it well, the way the birth of a first child is often predicted to be hard and long rather than a pleasant experience.

I tried many beginnings for my first novel, *The Truth About Family*. I also tried out the same beginning in many different forms, attempting various voices. I spent a long time contemplating whether to use or discard the prologue; then I tried to squeeze the backstory and the inciting incident into the same first page of Chapter 1.

I started feeling desperate after writing and rewriting the first couple of chapters of my book. It looked like I would never be able to begin at the beginning, since it appeared so terrible to me. Or at least not "brilliant" enough.

What helped me (since you have probably already surmised that I did finish *The Truth About Family*), and what made that project very special, then and now, was this: continue writing the story.

My solution might not work for everyone, but it was ideal for me.

I wrote further mostly because I promised others that I would keep the story going. I promised it to three people, two of my beta-readers, who were reading my book chapter-by-chapter, as well as my writing teacher, dear friend, and best-selling author, Menna van Praag, whose monthly international teleseminars I was been participating in through the year 2014.

At some point during my continued writing, I forgot all about the bad beginning and the bad first chapter. And at the most unexpected moment, the bad-hook-dilemma resolved all by itself. Here is how it happened.

During those international writing seminars with Menna, I submitted three pages for her review. In one particular session, I sent her three first pages of what was, at that time, Chapter 9 of my book.

Menna returned to me a written review with praise and constructive critique. But the lightbulb went off for me during the phone session with all nine of the participants. As Menna commented on my contribution, I learned something extraordinary and very personal. I experienced what a great hook meant for me, how it felt and how I could recognize it in my writing.

Menna said, "I really enjoyed your three pages." And then she said something which I recall almost word-for-word as I write this article, more than two years later. Menna asked, "Why don't you start your book with this chapter? You don't have to build the book sequentially along a timeline. You can come to the 'start' of the story later."

I felt a wave of recognition shower over me. Here's why.

This particular phone session was my *second* with Menna. For the first class, I had sent her Chapter 1 and for the second, Chapter 9. I had left *seven* chapters in-between untouched. I had looked through them, but I hadn't been drawn to revise them or send any of them to Menna. Instead, I let myself be guided by, what I call now, my "fun-detecting antenna" and chose Chapter 9. In retrospect, I now see that I chose it and no other chapter because it was the most fun to edit and prepare for Menna's review.

A year after that fateful seminar, I read an article by Rachel Aaron called "How I Went From Writing 2,000 Words a Day to 10,000 Words a Day."* This article addressed her productivity as a writer. One of the three criteria that best enhanced her productivity and increased her word count reminded me of my "hook-experience."

Here is what Rachel wrote in the section of her article titled "Side 3: Enthusiasm":

"Those days I broke 10k were the days I was writing scenes I'd been dying to write since I planned the book. They were the candy bar scenes, the scenes I wrote all that other stuff to get to. By contrast, my slow days (days where I was struggling to break 5k) corresponded to the scenes I wasn't that crazy about.

This was a duh moment for me, but it also brought up a troubling new problem. If I had scenes that were boring enough that I didn't want to write them, then there was no way in hell anyone would want to read them. This was my novel, after all. If I didn't love it, no one would.

…

This discovery turned out to be a fantastic one for my writing. I trashed and rewrote several otherwise perfectly good scenes, and the effect on the novel was amazing. Plus, my daily word count numbers shot up again because I was always excited about my work. Double bonus!"

As I wrote the first draft of this chapter, I reviewed those old submissions to Menna's writing seminars and found out that even before reading Rachel's article and after the revealing lesson with Menna, I had intuitively done the same. Just like Rachel, I let myself be led by my enthusiasm.

Here is what happened during the third seminar with Menna. I made the old Chapter 1 into the new Chapter 2, after the famous and by now treasured Chapter 9. As I let myself contemplate this episode a bit, I recognized that its start was slow because it was rather melancholic. Later in the chapter was good and also engaging, but the start was dragging because the protagonist was going, with his head hanging low, to the school master's office.

So I asked myself what could have happened before? Well, he was apparently sent to the director's office. But by whom, and where was he before that? That led to a dynamic and exciting scene between adolescents bickering with each other (or rather one bickering with the protagonist). This new dialogue suddenly showed some features of my characters, especially the protagonist, features that I had originally tried to unravel in the seven chapters between Chapter 1 and Chapter 9, but hadn't been able to until that moment. Here was a clear "Show - don't tell!" And I had found it just by identifying what made me enthusiastic when I revisited that chapter.

So I followed my *fun-detecting antenna* again. Even for the chapter that I initially thought was bad and boring.

This *fun-detecting antenna* helped me write a highly-praised hook for my second book right from the start. Menna suggested that I test it out, try starting the book with another scene. But after doing so, it became obvious that the latter wasn't working. The first solution was clearly better.

All these experiences following Menna's advice to experiment and discover how my *fun-detecting antenna* functioned were and still are amazing. Sometimes I forget and force myself to write something I have started but that clearly isn't flowing and doesn't work. But I discover more and more often, just like Rachel Aaron did for her word count, that

the fun factor isn't a bonus, it's a must.

Quality is the outcome when an author puts her whole self, including the heart, soul and best of the brain into her work.

Dear friends, if you have any remote fun reading this book, then you can be assured, and have probably already suspected by now, that the choice of topics and writing of the chapters, were done by following my *fun-detecting antenna.*

What kind of signal does your *fun-detecting antenna* receive right now regarding your work-in-progress and writing in general?

References in this chapter:

* http://www.sfwa.org/2011/12/guest-post-how-i-went-from-writing-2000-words-a-day-to-10000-words-a-day/

I – Ideas and Inspiration

"Where do you get your ideas from?" I've read this question in a couple of articles and even found a version of it in the title of a book series for writers.

I've been asked this question as well.

The first impulse is often to say "I've no idea where my ideas come from."

That would be probably the most accurate answer, but I'm aware that saying it might not be very well received.

So, as I often do when in doubt, I decided to consult a dictionary.

Here are the definitions of the words *idea* and *inspiration* I found in Cambridge Dictionaries Online.*

An *idea* is:

- *"a suggestion, thought, or plan*

- *knowledge or understanding about something*

- *a belief about something*

- *a purpose or reason for doing something"*

and *inspiration* is:

- *"someone or something that gives you ideas for doing something*

- *a sudden good idea*

- *someone that people admire and want to be like"*

I think I have experienced and tapped from all of these definitions when I write or create something. And that applies to all areas of my life, both private and business. Including cooking, drawing with my children, cleaning the house, writing commercial offers, updating my website, writing application letters, business emails, etc.

But somehow when it comes to writing (my books, articles, guest blog posts) I sometimes catch myself being afraid that I will run out of ideas too soon or only come up with the wrong ones that nobody will like.

So far, that hasn't happened, but this fear comes up, especially when I am about to finish a project. Thoughts then run in my head like hamsters on a wheel. *What will come next? What if I don't get any new ideas?* These unsettling thoughts make their appearance in various shapes and colors again and again, even when an army of other already-existing creative ideas and partially-begun projects are waiting for their turn to arrive.

It might be procrastination or running away from what I have to do at the current moment, but my brain tries to figure out over and over how ideas are generated inside it. Sometimes, guided by this fear, I even try to collect ideas. I have bought books of writing prompts, gathered quotes, tagged hundreds of links on my browsers' favorites bar with all kind of great ideas to inspire me. Do I use any of them? Yes, I do. But only a small percentage. And as time progresses, I look less and less at those collections.

So where then do I *mainly* tap my ideas from? The answer is, in fact, very simple. From all the passion ignited in me by being in the current moment. For example, if I am chatting with a person and listen to that person from his or her point of view, then the combination of what this person shares with me and all my past experiences as I perceive them now, ignites a bright fire of curiosity. The same happens when I create on my own in the quietness of my home during working hours or nights. Reading books, emails, surfing online or just re-reading the end of a chapter I have written the day before, all of these are able to spark a new idea – one born out of all gathered experiences and something I can't explain but which many call imagination. But this fire is only ignited when I am fully present and not lost in my thoughts about the past or future. If I am lost in anxious thoughts, then nothing happens. No fire, no warmth.

So the question is, do we really need to understand the mechanisms of idea-generation and inspiration processes? Or is it just about diving into them and getting inspired by surrounding us world, the circumstances we are in and all that we have gathered on our way so far?

It is impossible not to analyze and try to understand everything – though most of us try to and unsuccessfully so – and I realize more and more often that a spark of an idea, process or inspiration are as much a miracle as the conception and birth of a child. There might be certain biological processes to both, but you will never know when and how the fertile ground you provide will generate an idea or a child.

So what remains? What shall we do if we can't control this process?

The answer might sound both relieving and terrifying: *Nothing.*

Here are some questions for your contemplation: Do you agree that ideas and inspiration are uncontrollable and simply visit us as some kind of angels or aliens? Or do you think that there is a logical and easily understandable process to all the ideas your brain generates? Can you control them and do you believe there is a need for such control? Or should we all just witness the process, enjoy it, as well as tap energy and magic from it?

References in this chapter:

* http://dictionary.cambridge.org/

J – Justification, Judgment, and Joy

Have you ever felt a need to justify what you are doing? Even if no one asked or questioned it?

I definitely did. And sometimes still do. We probably all do this when we feel insecure or when we fear that others might judge us for what we do.

In my case, this is particularly true of writing. Since I don't earn a living from my writing yet, I sometimes catch myself trying to hide the act of writing when somebody calls me during the day and asks what I am doing at that moment. Then I say, "I am working." I don't say, "I'm working on my book" or "I am writing right now." And even when I say it, I may immediately start adding something to justify why I do it.

Writing is part of my business now, so this is what I do and should do during the day, or at least during a part of the day. Still, I sometimes have the idea that if I don't earn my full living from it, then I am not successful and therefore shouldn't do it.

What is interesting is that when I am insecure, then what others say in return sounds like judgment to me. In fact, I discovered myself expecting judgments in those moments and becoming defensive. Even positive and encouraging messages do not sound comforting to me, but judgmental instead.

Around the time when I first wrote this chapter, I said to a friend, "I'm having the best time of my life right now – regarding being fulfilled in a job – but I'm afraid to feel happy about it."

Then a few days later I took part in a discussion on one of my favorite blogs, "The Kill Zone" (TKZ),* which is authored, hosted and maintained by a group of well-known and experienced mystery writers. The discussion took place in the comment section of one of the "Reader's Friday" posts when the readers of the blog (many of whom are writers themselves) were asked to share their experiences as writers. On that particular Friday, April 15, 2016, to be precise, James Scott Bell, one of my favorite authors on the subject of writing craft and writing as a business, asked the blog readers whether we would take a million dollars if someone would have offered it in exchange for never writing fiction again. Would we accept or reject? And if we would agree, what would we do with that million dollars?**

I was the first to comment because being in Europe, I was probably one of the first to read the post and the notification about it, which usually comes to my inbox in the early afternoon when most people in the USA – and most TKZ readers – are still sleeping.

I said that *No*, I would not accept the million. My answer was based on my current circumstances as well as having learned from many experiences of denying myself my heart's desires.

An exciting discussion developed afterward. Many of the contributors said that they would take the million because they had a family to care for. Some stated that they would take the million and find another genre of writing to pursue, such as non-fiction. One writer said she would open a publishing house. Most said that in one way or another they would not leave the world of writing and publishing entirely. Some stated that they would continue writing fiction for themselves, ask a friend or a family member to publish their story under their names, or in some other way "sneak" their fiction into the world. Less than a handful said that they would say *No*.

Initially, I also almost said *Yes*, that I would take the million and stop writing fiction. And my intention was dictated by the same reasons that most of the writers had given for why they would take it – to fulfil obligations and take care of family.

But as I let myself contemplate the topic and consult my true feelings, as well as quieting the fear and the voices shouting, *This is what you are supposed to say!* I heard another voice. A quiet one. The one which is nurtured through the feeling of joy. The joy of writing, the joy of being with my husband and my children, as well as with extended family and friends.

It posed a question to me, *Do I need a million of dollars or do I need to enjoy mine and my family's lives to best take care of those I love?*

The answer was a heartfelt *No* to the first half and *Yes* to the second half of the question. The million dollars was not necessary. But being fully here and enjoying what I already have in my life was.

Another lightbulb switched on a moment later. Most parents say they want their children to follow their dreams. We, today's parents, were often asked as children, "Who do you want to become when you grow up?" and were nurtured and helped to go in the directions of our dreams. Until the moment arrived to choose the direction of our studies at a college or university. That is where many parents used to and often still do drop a "bomb." Many, intentionally or otherwise, communicate the following, "Choose a job that will bring money and sustain both you and your future family. Choose a job that brings a secure work situation and salary. Don't choose the unsure way of an artist. Choose your brain over your heart."

I don't blame the generation before us, because they learned the same from their parents. The secure and more reasonable jobs changed based on the time period our ancestors lived in. In 17th and 18th centuries, the arts were considered more appropriate for a girl from a wealthy family to learn. Today, arts are considered more insecure in terms of financial stability for any gender.

But what about the heart? Why don't we let ourselves be driven by it? Or by the joy our heart's desires produce when we carry them out? Are taking care of loved ones and others and following one's heart mutually exclusive? Won't I best teach my children to follow their dreams if I follow mine, and support them in theirs when they start the exciting adventure of learning a profession and trying things out?

I enjoyed each of the occupations I tried out. And I tried many of them. You can see them reflected in my bio at the end of this book and on its back cover. I also moaned about each of them, loving them in certain circumstances and less in others. In retrospect, I realize that it was life itself, *my* life, who helped and still helps me to find the best way for me.

So perhaps there is no need to discuss the value of a million of dollars, whether I (or others) would take it in exchange for writing or not, and whether there is value in accepting it or not. What matters is this moment of now and how I handle it. That's all.

I would like to challenge you to open your hearts and your brains and look "inside."

Consider and answer the following questions: When are you the most creative? When do you dive under the comfortable duvet of complaints and worries, or when are you out of your comfort zone, feeling the chill of the unknown on your arms and spine?

Remember, discomfort and confusion can be a sign that you are about to experience something exciting, that you are about to break out of your same old box of worries, complaints, and procrastination. What if those strange feelings of discomfort and confusion are indicators that you might be living an exciting life and are ready to "bungee jump" into your heart's desire?

I wish you joyful "bungee jumping" into your dreams and passion!

References in this chapter:

* https://killzoneblog.com/

** https://killzoneblog.com/2016/04/reader-friday-would-you.html

K – Knowledge

Writers often hear both:

- *"Write what you know."*

- *"When you write, don't limit yourself to what you know."*

As in anything, we humans try to prove one side or another.

I've read numerous articles on both sides and can resonate with many of them. So I wondered whether the disagreement might lie in the way we define knowledge.

I looked into one of my palm-size thesauri for help and found the following synonyms for the word *knowledge*:

*"Enlightenment, erudition, wisdom, science, information, learning, scholarship, lore, and also understanding, discernment, perception, apprehension, comprehension, judgment."**

I had to read this twice. These words didn't define the absolute term that I thought *knowledge* to be. Initially, I thought what I learned in school, at the university, at work, as well as at home, was what I knew. Of course, I realized later that this was all influenced by the culture I grew up in. In my case, it was colored by the Soviet Moldova, the Soviet Union in general, Algeria, and then Moldova after the collapse of the Soviet Union, Germany, Denmark, as well as handful other countries, which I visited during vacations and business trips. And indirectly also by countries, where dear-to-me family members, friends and other people in my life came from or lived in.

As I contemplated what my knowledge was based on, I realized that the synonyms above very much reflected what it was, including learning, perception, apprehension, and judgment.

To make sure I was on the right track, I took a look at another palm-size dictionary, this time for a definition, and found the following:

"Knowledge:

1. *Knowing about things*

2. *Information*

3. *All a person knows*

4. *All that is known."***

Then came a list of synonyms, and I read the following words:

*"Awareness, cognition, comprehension, consciousness, familiarity, grasp, insight, know-how, understanding, experience, expertise, proficiency; as well as data, facts, information, intelligence."***

That made the meaning of knowledge even broader.

I've had the pleasure of talking to aspiring writers about what it means to write what you know in fiction. That was in the beginning of March 2016 as part of the Creative Writing Camp organized by the South Gate Society School of Creative Writing.***

As I explored the writing of others and my own in preparation for the workshop I would be leading, I realized that knowledge comprises both what we have learned *and* our current interests, what makes us curious. We filter most of the other things out and concentrate on those which are of interest to us. And this is how our knowledge is shaped. By experiencing and mixing new with old, strange with familiar, odd with comfortable.

But there is another aspect to knowing. Something interesting happens when the words *write* and *know* switch places in ***"Write what you know."*** The sentence becomes ***"Know what you write."***

In August 2014, I had an "Aha!" moment, which still feels like a secret not open to many. I was one of the callers on the internet radio show *Being Here* hosted by Ariel and Shya Kane.**** As we discussed the question I put to them, Shya said something that still sounds for me very fresh and new when I think of it. He said that he *liked* taking responsibility for how he reacted toward others, as well as for his life in general.

That was very new to me. Up to that moment, I used to think that responsibility was a burden. But at the same time, I loved being in control of my life. What Shya said was very intriguing and simultaneously made sense for the first time. ***That taking responsibility could be fun.***

So I started testing it out and with every step, I found confirmation of this concept. It is fun and I am in control. I don't have to blame others for what I do or how I feel about how my life is turning up. It is sometimes easier and more comfortable to blame someone or something for my discomfort, but these complaints do not help to gain comfort. Only taking responsibility and coming back into the current moment of my life does.

Later, I discovered the same could be true about writing. In an article about writing fiction based on a true story, by an author whose name I don't remember anymore, the author said that if a change to actual historical events is made, then this change should be done deliberately, with full intention and will.

That reminded me of my conversation with Ariel and Shya about taking responsibility for what I am doing and for the results of my actions. I realized that even if characters do take over some of the control in my books, as they should, I can still put them into specific time and situations. I am setting up the environment and the framework – just like in a computer game, the characters act as players inside that game.

Or like in a board game, we, the writers, make a move and see what happens, then we adjust our strategy and make another move. All the while taking the responsibility and at the same time having fun doing it.

All this *knowledge* is know-how, understanding, proficiency, facts, perception and so much more.

So let's not analyze what we know or don't know, but just embrace and enjoy what we observe – without labeling it as good or bad, as too much or not enough – and realize that our knowledge changes in every moment just as much as we do.

References in this chapter:

* *Random House Thesaurus*, 2nd edition, 1995

** *Oxford Mini-Reference Dictionary and Thesaurus*, 1st Edition, 1995

*** http://www.thesouthgatesociety.com/

**** http://www.transformationmadeeasy.com/being-here-radio-show/

L – Life, Libel, and Liability

Since the chapters titles in this book follow the letters of the alphabet, almost every time I began writing a new chapter, I searched in various glossaries first for words starting with that next letter.

Liability caught my eye when I looked for words starting with an *L*. I wondered how I could I write something cheerful and motivational for my fellow writers about *liability*.

The word life, I thought, *is different. You can show positive things about life, but how do you show something positive about* liability?

It was an interesting challenge. And both words *life* and *liability* started dancing in my head.

At first, I didn't know how to approach these two notions. A wish to address them, as well as thoughts of taking responsibility for what we do as writers, began to emerge, just as it did when I wrote the chapter about *knowledge* (see the previous Chapter "K – Knowledge").

But there was something else coming to the surface too, something that was important to me and where I felt I had relevant experiences to share, but I still couldn't identify quite what it was. So I continued researching.

I looked into *Creative Writing: A Guide and Glossary to Fiction Writing* by Collin Bulman, which is also structured in alphabetical order and where I regularly searched for inspiration for the chapters of the book in your hands.

From all the words starting with an *L* that Collin Bulman addressed, only the word *libel* related in any way to the word *liability*. I had heard of libel before, as well as the seriousness involved, so I began to read the article somewhat reluctantly.

As I read on and thought a bit longer about libel (and why I seemed not to be able to let this word alone), I understood that it was a missing link in the chain I had created between the words *life* and *liability*.

I realized that this surfacing and important topic, which was especially important to me in 2013 when I was exploring what it meant to write my first book, was the fear that my writing could be considered by someone as libelous.

So I followed the advice given by Natalie Goldberg in her famous quote (see Chapter B – Book). In other words, I let myself "be split open," and started writing the story which, at that time, stirred me the most. I told the truth in those bits that exposed the genuine story behind *The Truth About Family*. But even then, I was still utterly scared to be judged and feared that someone would claim that I had defamed them or a person close to them.

This fear even kept me from writing, or at least slowed down the creation of the book considerably. But as I took a step backward and considered the whole situation non-judgmentally, this fear spurred me to ask myself why the writing of this book was so important to me? What did I want to achieve by writing a book about my father and his story?

The answers were revealing and uplifting. I wanted to show – especially to my dad's grandchildren (my sister's daughter and my own children), who never had a chance to meet him in person – what made my father the wonderful person that those who knew him claimed him to be. And all this included his challenging childhood as an orphan of World War II and as an individual who faced bitter rejections in his life.

I discovered that writing this book was not about assigning guilt for those words and events that had cut deeply into his soul and heart and stopped him in the search for his family. No, I realized that there were also people who welcomed him, who pushed him forward and helped him along the way so that he could study at a university and succeed in life. That there were also people who made him feel at home, who made it possible for him to spend the holidays – time meant to be spent in a family – with their own wonderful family, and ultimately create a family of his own, the one I was lucky enough to be born into.

No, I wasn't after a documentary, I was after "resurrecting" my father's kind heart, which I was fortunate to get to know and remember from my early years.

This goal helped me shape the characters and also choose a photograph of my father for the cover. It also helped me keep some of those uncomfortable events in the story because they contributed to shaping my dad's character and the way he went through his life. And it helped me gain at least some understanding of how those uncomfortable events could have happened, and insight into the people who induced them.

While I was still finishing my first book, I began writing my second book, *A Spy's Daughter*, which is entirely fictitious but uses a lot of true events from my life. These truths are wildly mixed with quirky bits of imagination, similar to how LEGO® building blocks can be put together into something completely new by adding colorful bricks from other sets.

And I realized something else, which was confirmed by the reviews and opinions my first two books received. I learned that there is a balancing act between writing what I know and taking care that my writing doesn't offend anyone. This balance made my books better because it removed any bitterness or anger I felt toward those things that I didn't prefer, in both the past and the present.

The act of writing and of taking care of people (both others and myself) during the writing process, helped me stop moaning about the fact that my father died, or about any other "misfortunes" in my life. Instead, the conscious process of putting words on paper and weighing what they might mean for the readers and me, helped me tap into enriching moments of support and inspiration.

In both my fiction and non-fiction, writing down the truth, being kind, and allowing the many inspiring people in my life to support me helped me find my mission. And find what I wanted to be remembered for. I discovered that I wanted to be thought of and remembered as *Optimist Writer*.

But what will I do if someone feels offended by my words? If someone wants to hold me liable for what I have written? Honestly, without the particulars, I don't know what I will do. But I do know that I will try to be attentive and compassionate to the wishes and feelings of others, as well as to my own truth. I will ultimately let life lead me and show me the way.

Some questions for contemplation: What are your experiences with writing your truth and taking care of people so that no-one sees your writing as libel? What balancing acts have you done in your writing? And how did this creative discomfort feel for you?

M – Magic

(or Remembering What Started the Realization of a Dream)

As many parents do, my husband and I read bedtime stories to our children. Sometime during May 2016, I read Cinderella to my then five-year-old son, Niklas, and recalled that the fairy tale had a special meaning for me. I mentioned this to my son, and after reading it to him, I told him why the story (or rather one of the films based on it) helped me officially start my writing career.

Here is how I started my very first blog post back in 2013:

"Those of you who grew up in the former Soviet Union will remember the old film version of Cinderella from 1947. If I am not mistaken, it was first produced in black-and-white and later in color. I think that it is the best production of Cinderella ever. But I guess everyone thinks this of their favorite movies from childhood. The reason I mention this is that in the film, the most amazing wonders are not only performed by the Fairy Godmother but also by her page, who was at the same

*time her pupil and whose name was simply 'Boy.' Every time he was told to work a miracle, he looked apologetically at Cinderella and said, 'I am not a wizard, I am just learning!' and then did the most beautiful things.**

*So, now you know: I am not a wizard or a fairy, I am just learning. I am learning to create magic with words."***

Starting my very first blog was a huge adventure and daring for me. Even four years later, after having published eight books, offering two more on my site, this book here, and with five more on the way, I still consider myself an apprentice in writing. Even more so back then, when I thought I was crazy to dare to write and share my writing.

That is why the headline of my very first blog said, "I am not a writer, I am just learning." A short time later, I changed it to "I am not a wizard, I am just learning."

Early on, my friends and family read and sent me their feedback on my blog posts. And I found new and dear to me friends through my blog, as you learned in "Introduction (Part 2) – The Story Behind This Project" at the beginning of this book.

Here is what my dear friend and writing teacher Menna van Praag told me about my first blog and its original headline, as we chatted during a break at a transformational seminar with Ariel and Shya Kane in April 2013 in Hamburg, Germany. Menna said that she very much liked what she had read so far, but there was something with which she didn't agree. And she let me know what that was.

She didn't agree with the headline. "But you are a writer! And a magician," she said, "You create magic with words."

Menna's words made me catch my breath. Soon after that, my website's new headline read, "Creating magic with words."

Fast forward three years, to my son's bedroom. Sitting with Cinderella's tale on my lap, I had to smile at how childishly proud I was to tell this story of my writing dream to my son, and how he smiled at me very much like parents would at children proudly showing off their drawings.

This experience reminded me of how I sometimes worry if my writing endeavor is worthwhile to follow, whether or not it is a waste of time to chase one's dream.

I love what I do and my day is not complete if I haven't written something new, however little it may be.

Still, the fear was there. *Have I chosen the correct path? What if people criticize me?*

Some dreams are right for some people, I continued thinking, and the same dreams might be utterly foolish for others. Am I, a non-native to the primary languages I speak, not a fool to write and publish in English, or in any language for that matter? Am I not a fool to chase a dream of being a writer?

And then, when I recall publishing my very first piece of writing, the reactions to it and to my subsequent creations, I realize that I'm not chasing my dream, I am *living* it. Right now, in this very moment.

In the process of writing this chapter, I recalled a trinket I bought for myself several years ago to remind me that I am living my writing dream. It is a chain and a locket in the shape of a little book, with the words "FAIRY TALE" written in capital letters on its cover. I wear this chain and the pendant nearly every day, although with time I had forgotten the reason I bought it and what had inspired me to buy it.

Putting together this chapter and thinking about what the magic of writing means for me suddenly brought it all back.

I saw this locket in a jewelry shop at the Copenhagen international airport, right after I had written down a couple of pages for my first novel while waiting for my plane home. As soon as I saw this metal bead shaped like a tiny book, I thought, *Wow, I am writing a book. I am a writer. I can't believe this. That is a fairy tale!*

So I live my fairy tale now.

And when I am self-editing, I am separating ashes from lentils.

I am not at the "And they lived happily ever after" yet because this would mean being at the end of my fairy tale.

Do I want this?

No!

Right now, I will just enjoy every moment, whether it is removing the ashes or dancing at a ball.

A few questions for you to contemplate upon: What reminds you of how you started writing? What inspired and helped you to put your first stories, articles, blog posts into words?

References in this chapter:

* Here is a short synopsis from Wikipedia (https://en.wikipedia.org/wiki/Cinderella_(1947_film)) of the Soviet version of Cinderella:

"Cinderella (Russian: Зóлушка, translit. Zolushka) is a 1947 Soviet musical film by Lenfilm studios.

It is a classical story about Cinderella, her evil Stepmother, and the Prince, but told with caustic satirical undertones by the Soviet writers Evgeny Schwartz and Nikolai Erdman. Many phrases from the movie became aphorisms.

Yanina Zhejmo played young Cinderella while being 38 years old."

** http://victoriaichizlibartels.com/about-this-blog-and-its-title/

N – Novels, Novellas, Novelettes, and Short Stories

It's quite curious how unsure in ourselves most of us human beings are. I guess I am not alone in having specific ideas of what I am *not* able to do, and being sure that those "non-abilities" are more significant than my abilities.

For me, in respect to my writing, these thoughts have been progressive.

First, I thought I couldn't write a book. Then when I wrote my first book, I was delighted to have reached the word count that could classify it as a novel. I have reached 55,000 words. Wow! I hadn't reached 100,000 yet, as many novels by famous contemporary authors often did. But I was an apprentice, wasn't I?

To my utter horror, on April 29, 2015, only one month after self-publishing my novel, I read an article "Shorter is better" by Joe Moore on The Kill Zone blog* saying that novels started at about 60,000 words. *Oh no!* I thought. *My first self-published novel was a mere novella!*

I have even expressed my dismay openly. Here is a comment I posted in response to Joe's article:

"Oops, so my first novel is a novella. I thought that novels start with 50,000. I have 55,900. But I guess the count does not matter very much.

I found very interesting what was said some time ago that a novella has only one plot-line and not several as a novel would have.

What I found with my writing is that I just go ahead and write (or plot) and the story develops itself into something, whether short or long. One short story I planned turned out to become a novel. And now I need to do a lot of additional research, but it is definitely worth it. Or the novel that I am writing now turned out to be a series, probably of novellas, because it contains separate stories and plots. So far five are planned. Who knows, maybe more are to come.

I guess the surprise the stories bring with them is one of the most exciting aspects of writing."

As you can see, I did try to calm myself down and silence my thoughts claiming that shorter works of fiction were of less quality than longer pieces.

Here is what Joe Moore answered to my comment,

"Victoria, unless your publishing contract specifies a definite word count, just write the best story you can. That's all that matters."

I was delighted for such motivation and replied,

"Thank you for answering my comment, Joe. I'm a self-publisher. So I have a contract with myself. I am learning to be less critical every day. ;)"

But even Joe's reassuring comment and my own attempts to be kind to myself didn't reduce the fear of being worse than others because I was not able to write pieces longer than around 50,000 words.

So the next step was to find excuses. *Short stories were not for me.* They were reserved for special masters. Who could possibly repeat the famous 6-word-long short story by Hemingway? *No.* Such apprentices like me shouldn't even try to write one. (A side note here: by this time, I had written and published a couple of short stories on my blog. Which got favorable comments. But my "brainy" brain knew better, of course.) As to novels, I decided that I didn't like reading long descriptions. *I prefer reading novellas*, I thought, trying to ignore the short stories, novels, and epics I'd read and loved (including many with brilliant, long descriptions; see Chapter "D – Descriptions"). *All these are exceptions!* my brain shouted. *I am more into novellas!*

And on and on this went. But not all the time.

It was again Instantaneous Transformation,** an amazingly effective, efficient and kind approach developed by Ariel and Shya Kane, which helped me to shed light on what was going on. I realized that these thoughts came when I wasn't writing. When I was actually putting my stories on paper or my computer screen, I didn't hear them. I supposed that I had them, but the stories seemed to sweep me away from my worries.

In one of the 'video mini-sessions' they share once a month on their website and Facebook page, Ariel and Shya pointed out that it could be valuable to notice having these thoughts, because sometimes they come unnoticed and draw us away from the current moment of our lives, increasing the feelings of stress and discomfort. If we notice them, without judging what we see, we can find our way back to the current moment and to being truly alive.

Sure enough, the more attention I paid the more I started noticing these thoughts also during my writing process. I observed how my hands hovered over the keyboard without typing, how I worried whether a particular story or article would be good enough, or liked or appreciated by its readers.

The final exposure of the complete untruth of those thoughts claiming that books of shorter length were of lesser quality, or that they were solely a product of modern times (and thus having me being attached to them), was when I opened Colin Bulman's *Creative Writing: A Guide and Glossary to Fiction Writing* (mentioned several times before in this book). In the article titled "Novella and Novelette," Colin wrote:

"The following are some notable novellas:

● *Truman Capote, Breakfast at Tiffany's (1958)*

- *Joseph Conrad, The Heart of Darkness (1902)*

- *Ernest Hemingway, The Old Man and the Sea (1952)*

- *Aldous Huxley, The Genius and the Goddess (1955)*

- *Franz Kafka, Metamorphosis (1915)*

- *George Orwell, Animal Farm (1945)*

- *Robert Louis Stevenson, The Strange Case of Dr. Jekyll and Mr. Hyde (1886)*

- *H.G. Wells, The War of the Worlds (1898)"*

This list was the final pinprick needed to let the hot air out of my balloon full of worries about the length of my writing pieces.

But what shall I do with all the time I have now that these concerns have disappeared? I guess I could use it for some creativity instead.

Questions to you: What thoughts about writing fill the space when you don't write? Regarding word counts, have you ever considered or judged in any way the length of your stories? Do you think there must be standard lengths for particular types of stories or articles, or does a standard establish itself, which is what happened for me when writing the chapters of this book, each one turning out to be around 1,000 words without any planning beforehand?

References in this chapter:

* https://killzoneblog.com/2015/04/shorter-is-better.html

** http://www.transformationmadeeasy.com/

O – Origin, Originality and the Art of Being Authentic

Two of my favorite writers have addressed the topic of being original and authentic.

Menna van Praag, in one of her one-minute writing courses on Facebook,* shared how in her twenties she desperately tried to write something original and didn't manage to, and how with time she discovered that most authors, including Shakespeare, "stole" plots and stories and re-told them in their own authentic way.

Here is what Elizabeth Gilbert wrote in her book *Big Magic: Creative Living Beyond Fear* in the chapter "Originality vs. Authenticity":

"… the older I get, the less impressed I become with originality. These days, I'm far more moved by authenticity. Attempts at originality can often feel forced and precious, but authenticity has quiet resonance that never fails to stir me.

Just say what you want to say, then, and say it with all your heart.

Share whatever you are driven to share.

If it's authentic enough, believe me – it will feel original."

These words are very inspiring. I can relate to her experiences. And I am sure other authors and their favorite artists can relate to them too.

But how do you define authenticity? Without looking in a dictionary, I mean. Hoes does it feel to be authentic? What does the "quiet resonance of authenticity" mean for me? What do I *really* want to say?

For quite some time I thought that my past had hindered my ability to say what I wanted. That I had to leave it all behind, get rid of it to find my authenticity.

But somehow my past kept coming back, in one form or another, and very prominently in pieces I was writing.

My story and the stories of those I share my life with kept appearing in my blog posts in and my books. Yes, I learned to write what I know (see Chapter "K – Knowledge"), but wasn't it too arrogant to write so often about myself and those around me from my very close proximity?

Yes, I had heard many times that the way we are today is shaped by all that has happened to us. And I thought I agreed with this, but still, I couldn't understand or define with particular words what my authenticity was about.

The most inspiring to me was the aforementioned transformational approach by Ariel and Shya Kane –

which, with practice, I started to experience and grasp – especially their second principle of Instantaneous Transformation:

"No two things can occupy the same space at the same time."

What they mean by this is the fact that anyone in the world, including me, can only be as we are right now. That includes our past, our current thoughts and our aspirations for the future.

No explanation or definition for how we are being in the current moment is needed, or probably even possible. I am at the moment as I am. And in any previous moment, I was as I was. At the same time, I couldn't have been who I wasn't. If I wrote those words about my father, about myself in my fiction, the way I did, then this is the way those words were supposed to come out. And if I edited them afterward, that is how they were meant to be. Because things didn't go any other way than the way they did.

The same happened with this chapter here. I didn't plan it in detail before writing it. Its origins came from my experience moment to moment. I did contemplate a bit on the subject before I started to write, and originally, I was going to address the word *onomatopoeia*. I discovered this word in Colin Bulman's *Creative Writing: A Guide and Glossary to Fiction Writing*, in the article titled, "Onomatopoeia." This word sounded quirky, and I do use a lot of sound-expressing words in my books. But when I started writing an article about onomatopoeia, it simply didn't work. After starting the article with a quote of Colin's and thinking for a couple of minutes on what to write, I decided to listen to the quiet voice wondering whether there was another term starting with *O*, which would work better for this chapter and which would be more fun for me to write about it. I gave it a try, and the word *origin* came first.

From there, a bridge to the phrase *originality* and *authenticity* appeared immediately, and I knew what I wanted to say.

But even then there was a surprise. As I began to write about authenticity, I thought that the word *origin* meant the places and events from before, from where I came from. But now, at the end of this article, I have a different sentiment. I feel that my most authentic expressions and creations can have their origin in so many places and events, whether experienced for the first time a second ago or from a long-ago-gathered memory, from the stories of those close to me, or people I met only recently. That is the brilliance of creativity – the most authentic and original expressions are often the most unexpected, first and foremost to ourselves.

Questions for you to contemplate upon: How do you experience authenticity? What does it mean for you? How does it feel when, upon reading your own writing, you have an urge to nod and say, "Yes, this is exactly what I wanted to say"?

References in this chapter:

*

https://www.facebook.com/mennavanpraag.mvp/videos/1061457853867012/

** *Practical Enlightenment,* Ariel and Shya Kane, 2015

P – Pace of a Story

Pace used to be the main criteria by which I judged the quality of a book I read, or pieces of that book. I realize now that I rarely said a book's particular topic didn't interest me. I usually said it was too slow.

Now, when I manage not to take my thoughts too literally or seriously, I am fascinated to realize that I perceive faster-flowing stories as better than "slower" ones.

Even when many (including me) agree that it is reasonable and healthy to slow down, the hurry of thoughts and the wish to get somewhere else other than where we are right now, seems to be a default programming of our brains. At least it appears to be the default program running inside my head. When a task is done (or maybe not even fully done yet), the question of *What next?* arises, faster and faster, until my brain can't deal with it anymore and it either explodes with frustration or leads me to sleep.

Is this how babies' brains function – absorbing as much information as they possibly can at a crazy pace, after which they need to take an extended break to process all of it? I often think that the smallest of humans are remarkably calm and slow and experience the world at a pleasant pace. But are they really? I guess, the exact answer will never be known, even if many scientists are of the opinion that the development of the human brain and the learning of new skills occurs in leaps rather than gradually.

Now, having two young children myself, I've learned that they grow most impatient and irritable when they are in the process of learning something substantially new. It makes sense, then, to give them time and space to complete that leap.

Hm, should I maybe allow that for myself too?

I've discovered that how I perceive a book depends on a number of things: the time of day I read it and on my state in general – whether I am tired at the end of a busy day or fresh in the morning with the first cup of espresso on the table in front of me. Even the same passages of the same book read differently at different times of day.

I now recall how I complained about the structure of the book *The Girl You Left Behind* by Jojo Moyes, which presented two stories with two main characters, and each story took place in a different timeframe. Reading in the evenings, I would complain how one chapter followed one storyline and the next jumped backward in time to follow the other storyline. Sometimes these jumps in time were even within the same chapter. And I thought I liked one of the two stories more than the other. But when I read the same book in the morning, I nodded with appreciation at how both stories and the structure of the book overall stirred and challenged me.

It was also in the mornings, that I liked reading both storylines and discovering the connections between them. I came to realize that I enjoyed the book only...when I gave myself time to read it without trying to hurry up and get to the end of it.

Is this what usually happens in the evenings? Our brains searching for an end, so that they can get some rest?

Recently, I read an article by Ariel and Shya Kane, whom I have quoted many times already in this book. In it, Ariel remembered how her family looked through the belongings of her grandmother, who had passed away some time earlier, and found a grocery shopping list from the day she died. Her grandmother had lived a fulfilled life, yet she still had a list of things she wanted to do on that last day. This story was incredibly touching and revealing. It showed me that there will always be things that I won't manage to complete. But this doesn't mean that something is incomplete in my life. Unless I perceive it as such.

For myself, I realize that I am capable of creating endless lists of what I could do and want to do. Curiously enough, I often want to have everything finished all at once. That is quite a quirky and naive paradox!

Another interesting thing I notice: when I complain about the pace of a book, there is usually something in my life that I am resisting and trying to process in my mind. When something in the book reminds me of that unresolved issue, I get stuck and struggle to get over it, blaming the source of the reminder for being too slow and not letting me get to the interesting bits. For example, that happened when I read Ariel and Shya Kane's book *Practical Enlightenment* for the first time.

While reading one of the chapters somewhere in the middle of the book, I heard myself thinking, *Oh, this bit is too slow. It lacks a story, an example. They only describe the challenges people face, but they should have written instead about a particular event that happened to them or other people to make the point stronger.*

Mind you, there *are* examples – tales and stories of real people – following and often preceding each point Ariel and Shya make in their book. But at some point, I had these thoughts again. After the second time, I stopped. *Wait for a second,* I said to myself. *What is happening here? Did Ariel and Shya's words maybe hit on something? Is there something I'm avoiding and those words simply stirred a sensitive cord?"*

I sighed bravely and said in my thoughts, *OK, let's check it.*

I reread those passages I had criticized in my head, and sure enough, there was an unresolved knot, a point where I felt vulnerable, where something inside me squeezed and felt uncomfortable. I tried to relax and consider the passages non-judgmentally. Funnily enough, it touched on a subject I had thought was resolved. I don't remember now what exactly that was, but I do recall that it was something I had thought I wasn't too sensitive about anymore. This little "complaining-about-pace-or-lack-of-a-story-incident" and the experiment of seeing what caused it was very revealing.

I am very grateful to have learned and been able to see that those complaints are neither good or bad. They are just indicators that I am off-balance and an opportunity to become aware of what is happening in that moment inside me. They might also be signs that a change is needed, either in thinking or activity.

Yes, these complaints also appear with books that don't interest me. But that doesn't mean that these books are bad. They are often perceived as great by other people. And thus, they are great. Just not for me. They are simply not what my heart wants to lead me to. So, why do I sometimes force myself to finish a book only to complain that it is bad? Why don't I leave that book in peace instead and turn my attention to a book or a story that would appeal to me?

My perception of the pace of a book is probably an indicator of the state of my mind at the given moment of reading it, what my expectations are of the given book, or even about something about myself I have yet to discover.

Realizing that also makes me understand different reactions toward my own books. I received various feedback toward the same book from different readers and editors. Some had only minor editorial notes to communicate, others said my book lacked description in places, that I had taken for granted that readers knew what I meant. Slowing down or even stopping and looking at my writing did the trick: I found out where it felt right to add more description and which bits I wanted to keep as they were. I also discovered that I could write pages of enjoyable description (see the Chapter "D – Descriptions") and have fun doing it.

So, what is the right pace for a story or a narrative in a book? Is there an absolute value? Or is it like riding a bike, going neither too slow nor too fast, adjusting the speed to the slope and the quality of the path, so that it can move along, without the cyclist falling and injuring herself? Yes, it is most probably like riding a bike, not only keeping it upright but also slowing down, pushing it up a hill, or even stopping and putting it away when it is time to take a break or when the path has ended.

The "road" of this chapter is ending now, and I have a few questions for you: What are you judging when you think of a book as being good or bad? Is it the pace of a story, its narrative, or something else? What is your state of mind when you enjoy the story and when you don't enjoy it that much? Does your reaction toward the story reveal something about yourself and your perception of the world around you? Do you read books only when you are in a certain state of mind or certain circumstances? If yes, what are they?

Q – Quantity and Quality

Quantity and *quality* are often used as opposed terms. Especially in writing, you've probably often heard people saying, "Quantity is not the same as quality."

On the other hand, you as a writer have most likely been motivated to write as much as you can. Maybe you've even been told that only by producing masses of material can you create brilliant pieces within it.

"You can't edit an empty page."

I love quoting this phrase again and again, though I haven't been able to find out who was the first to say it.

But what about already finished and published books. Which is better? Longer or shorter ones?

Like anything else, the relativity principle applies to both quantity and quality. There are brilliant epic novels and revealing short stories. The same goes for the badly written ones. You can find them in any length and genre.

Besides that, a book can be perceived by one person as good and sound awful to another.

So every writer needs to write his or her own perfect story, the one he or she wants to read. Most of us writers have heard this instruction many times.

We still need to improve and revise and let others edit and offer their opinion on what we have produced. But what if rewriting doesn't improve but simply changes the book? What if it is then neither better or worse but simply different?

Of course, there may be some people who think other than the way you do about your changes and rewrites. As in the case of a new software update, where the new functionalities replace the old ones you liked and used a lot. The new ones might be good or even better, but you don't feel like it is the case at the time.

When I wrote the Chapter "N – Novels, Novellas, Novelettes, and Short Stories" I realized that the length of a written piece didn't have much to do with its quality. So when thinking about quality in writing, I decided it would be a good idea to ask myself what advice I would give to my younger self, or to myself when I first started writing. Shaped somewhere between my heart and my brain, the following is what came to me:

If your inner critic or someone from the outside says to you that your book, or writing in general, is bad, then don't argue and don't defend yourself. That is a waste of your time and will only produce or increase the already-existing doubts about your work-in-progress or writing craft in general. And I suspect this is not the direction you want to take. Instead, tap into the power of your brain (or the brain of your critic) to boost your productivity and creativity.

Ask your mind or your external critic, "What is one little thing here that WE can do to make it better?" Yes, invite the one who critiques you (be it your brain or your friend) to be a part of your creative process. Then ask the question again and take the next little step on the way to improve your work-in-progress. Together, you and your critic (whether yourself or someone else), will manage so much more and so much better. You'll have a lot of fun, and if this is a friend or a family member, the whole process might bring you closer together than you could have ever imagined.

If you, on the other hand, are the one providing an opinion on the work of a fellow writer, then be as kind as you wish others to be to you. First of all, point out what you liked. Then say what you would improve. And always, always (!) provide a concrete suggestion for how to improve your colleague's work. Never critique without making specific recommendations for change. Let them know what you would do if this was your work-in-progress.

I once had an epiphany related to the above advice and about the topic of quantity versus quality.

I had the opportunity to ask a fellow independent writer for a review copy of their e-book. I chose the book because of its compelling description. It was relatively long, estimated by Amazon to be 480 pages.

I liked the main story a lot. And I also liked the side stories. But not the way they were woven together. The side stories sometimes distracted from the main one for too long. They started to become main stories of their own.

At first, I was afraid to comment on this book. I was afraid to offend the author. But then I wrote an email with my opinion and suggestions of what I would do to improve it, and the author appreciated it. I was surprised, but then I realized that I would have enjoyed it too.

This is what I realized about the experience, in regards to quantity and quality:

Telling several stories in parallel is risky. Even for masters like Jojo Moyes, whose book *The Girl You Left Behind* I mentioned in the previous Chapter "P – Pace of a Story." Her fascinating book lost me from time to time as a reader, or at least made me more impatient in the evening hours when I was already tired and wanted a story to sweep me away into its world. As I experienced it then, the multiple storylines got in-between one another, and it wasn't immediately apparent how they were connected. Some careful thinking and contemplating were needed to understand both stories. This contemplation was possible and pleasantly challenging in the mornings, with a cup of coffee in my hand, but not in the evenings when I wanted to relax from the busy day.

When reflecting on the story by the independent author mentioned above, I realized that I didn't want her to simply cut the subplots out of the story and make only the main one visible. Rather, I wanted her to enhance those side stories and dedicate whole books to them as well, create out of all that material a trilogy, a quartet, or a larger series of books.

It was an exciting discovery for me. The revision and adjustment of quantity to increase quality doesn't always mean cutting the word count down, as many authors suggest – among them Stephen King in his famous book, *On Writing: A Memoir of the Craft*. It can also – as I understand now – mean to add more material and restructure it in a way that makes the world of the story completely impossible to leave, at least not for a while.

I realize now that if I hadn't loved Jojo Moyes' other books before *The Girl You Left Behind*, I might not have finished reading this book. Yes, there were moments in the day when I loved the challenge she posed, but, in general, I enjoy being minimally challenged and not having to work hard to figure the story out.

I rarely dare to critique master authors and famous writers, yet strangely, in this article I managed to critique not only one of my favorite writers, but another accomplished author along as well. Though scary, I see that through this honesty I find my way in writing, at least the way that appeals to me right now. It might change in the future when I write other kinds of books, and I will be curious to discover the quantity and quality of them.

I have a suggestion. Let's not get intimidated by the word count. It doesn't matter that much. We can use quantity as a vehicle to achieve high quality. Quantity is not quality's enemy. By manipulating quantity in a particular and intentional way we can reach the quality we are aiming at.

A few questions for contemplation: Have you ever been critiqued about your word count (either internally by your brain or from the outside)? If yes, in what way? What do quantity and quality mean for you in writing and life in general? What are your experiences with reviews of your books? And what is your approach when you critique the writing of others?

R – Research

Like the other terms I've addressed in this cheerleading glossary for writers, *research* has numerous facets.

Research itself doesn't bring cherished words to paper or computer screen, but it can inspire their appearance and creation.

On the other hand, research can also "swallow" a writer and "save" her from writing or in other words help her to avoid the creative process, which is often longed-for but still quite unsettling.

Let's explore the topic of research using those mightiest of diagnostic tools, the seven key questions: *Who, What, Why, When, Where, How,* and *How much.*

Who should research?

Any writer (of course!), independent of the genre he or she is writing in. We will get more clues to this first question as we answer the others below.

What is research?

In Colin Bulman's *Creative Writing: A Guide and Glossary to Fiction Writing,* he says that,

"Readers expect the background to fiction to be accurate and authentic."

That, of course, applies even more to non-fiction. But also to fantasy and science fiction.

As the principal means of research, Bulman suggests reading, conducting interviews, corresponding, visiting various outdoor places and buildings, watching films and television, and searching the internet.

I surely agree. But I have also learned that reading books of the same genre, asking questions of others, corresponding and watching entertainment that informs the background of one's story might not be the only source for research and inspiration.

One of the greatest resources for me are books and articles on writing craft and the art of publishing. My background is in physics and engineering, and engineers often share solutions to the challenges they face with one another. They apply those solutions to the task at hand and create a new solution out of them. I have found this approach to be equally as effective and efficient for me as a writer.

As with anything else, there is no need to re-invent the wheel in writing. We can learn from other writers, review and appreciate what is available so far and then say, "Wow, that's great! What happens if I take this wheel, bend it until it is oval, and see how it functions in my seven-wheeled car of a story?"

We are all inspiring and can learn from each other, whether we are writers, engineers, doctors, homemakers, children, students, pensioners or of some other unique background.

Why research?

Bulman's quote above about accuracy and authenticity provides one answer to this question. There is also another possibility that comes to my mind. It is about having fun. To have fun, you simply have to keep on learning, finding and discovering something new. Continuously.

Let's come back to the second question in this list: what is research? Besides deepening the well of background information, research can also be a way to experiment with various storylines. Or it can mean actually doing what our characters do, for example flying a Spitfire, as the well-known British entertainer and children's writer David Walliams did for one of his latest books, *Grandpa's Great Escape.**

So, yes, this is why research is necessary. It lets us grow and learn new things, have fun and communicate our enjoyment to our readers.

When is research appropriate?

One could also ask here, "What exactly should a writer research and in what situation?"

I have discovered that for me the most critical point to put a manuscript aside and do some research is when the following thoughts appear in my head about a historical detail or a fact: *I got this. I don't have to double-check this. It's not that important anyway.* Especially when these thoughts become so loud in my head that I have to stop writing. At that moment, I know my brain is arguing with something authentic and true inside me that is eager to learn.

If, at that time, I wholeheartedly surrender and open a search window on the internet or take a book from my shelf, I often catch myself holding my breath, like I am about to find out a secret. However strange this may sound, I am sure that exactly this feeling is one of the things that keeps writers writing, researching and traveling around the world to find more exciting details for their stories. Sometimes, it even makes them go and do crazy things like having oneself arrested to see how it looks, feels and smells to be handcuffed and set in the back of a police car. Angela Ackerman did this** for *The Urban Setting Thesaurus: A Writer's Guide to City Spaces,* published in June 2016 with co-author Becca Puglisi.

Where can research be done?

Nowadays, research can be done anywhere. From home, while traveling, or in a setting created by yourself, whether virtually (with cards on an actual or virtual corkboard, filled with images and website links) or physically (by building an individual setting in one's garden). One of my greatest inspirations here is Nora Roberts. She uses all kinds of settings in her books and invents characters with an almost endless variety of backgrounds and moods. The places Nora describes in her books are inspired both by her life in her immediate vicinity and from afar. And if she doesn't have a particular setting, then she creates one of her own. She had a hotel built from a historical building in Boonsboro, the small town in Maryland where she lives. Having built the hotel, Roberts used the experiences she gathered during its design and construction in her romantic series, *Inn BoonsBoro Trilogy*. She also featured in it the pizzeria owned by her son, which is situated close to the hotel.

So, there are no limits on where to research. Of course, financial means can set some limits, but not necessarily. By using the methods mentioned above, you can still create or recreate a setting you are looking for without ever having been there.

One of the most memorable exercises for me was writing a story about a character who came from a country I had never been to before. I wrote this fictional piece about a man named Matti*** from Finland, shortly before I went on a business trip to Vaasa, a city on the west coast of Finland. I have written and shared many of my writing exercises on my blog, but this story was one of my favorites. I guess the challenge to research and write about something I knew absolutely nothing about beforehand was a big fun factor.

Photographs are also a special form of research for me. An exceptional place in my heart is occupied by the pictures from my father's childhood and youth, which I used as inspiration for *The Truth About Family* based on my dad's story. I carried copies of these photographs almost everywhere I went. I took them to help me answer the questions the story was posing. Sometimes the pictures asked questions that I answered by writing the story.

My bookshelves, filled among other with books on art and my collection of postcards and photographs, are one of my favorite places for research.

How to research?

I mentioned various methods of research above. But, ultimately, all of the questions and issues here can only be answered by a given author based on the needs of their story and their particular state of mind and circumstances. A pregnant writer, a mother of five children, a woman who never had children but wanted to, a father of a newborn, a parent who had lost a child to cancer, each one of these people would approach researching a childhood illness completely differently. With this in mind, a seemingly similar story can end up being vastly different, its light being broken through the individual prisms of an author's perspective and experiences.

How much or how long to research?

The short answer is, "As much as necessary, and as long as it is enjoyable and rewarding."

I would have argued with this reply in the past by saying, "But if it is so much fun, then you might get lost in research and never write again."

However, some time ago I discovered this latter statement to be untrue. At least untrue for me. When I studied a historical event for *The Truth About Family*, namely sending the first human into space on April 12th, 1961, I found myself consuming multiple articles and online videos. I couldn't seem to stop reading and watching all that material. One might think that I was deeply interested in this event and what happened, even if most of the details wouldn't move my story forward. But when I stopped and observed myself, I noticed that I wasn't actually having fun with that particular research anymore. I was merely afraid to take the next step and find out what the following scene would be.

Shortly after writing the first draft of the chapter you are reading now, I discovered this quote by Baltasar Gracián y Morales:

"Without courage, wisdom bears no fruit."

In other words, if research stalls and doesn't add to the gathered wisdom, if it stops being surprising or bringing discoveries along with it, in that case, it is high time to take courage, stop researching, and do the work.

What a great clue for determining when the answer we are after is found, and when to stop researching and come back to writing, isn't it!? Yes, fear and especially becoming aware of it can be a useful tool for discovering what is to be done next, and what is the best point in time for it to be done. To find the point of *now*.

Research is a mystery, just like the writing itself. The balancing act between the two is amazing, worth exploring and testing again and again.

A multi-dimensional question to you: What, why, when, where, how and how much do you research for your stories?

References in this chapter:

* http://www.boultbeeflightacademy.co.uk/single-post/2017/03/08/Grandpas-Great-Escape-david-walliams-spitfire-flight

** https://thewritingtrain.com/2016/06/08/one-the-train-with-angela-ackermann/

*** http://victoriaichizlibartels.com/matti/

S – Show Me What You've Got (or How a Writer Can Serve Others Without Putting Too Much Pressure on Herself)

As with almost any book on writing and its various facets, this one will also address the aspects of showing and telling. But it will approach *show* and *tell* from another angle.

During the first three years of my writing career and especially recently, I have come to realize that I joined an exotic species of the working population.

We, writers, want to write books that we would want to read. On the other hand, we also want others to love them.

Or we write motivational guide books to pull ourselves out of initially hopeless situations. At the same time, hoping these books will pull other people out of their miseries too.

What is interesting, though, is that whether others read our works or not, people survive without them. No one seems to need what we do for their daily and most urgent needs.

Also, we, who not only write but also love reading, don't (always) need the written word to survive physically. We do need it to enrich our lives, to decorate them. Just as paintings decorate our environments and make them a unique experience to be within.

Or like music and songs. Some time ago, I read about an exciting encounter of Elizabeth Gilbert with the famous songwriter Tom Waits. Here is what Liz (as Elizabeth Gilbert herself and her friends like to call her) writes in the Chapter "Tom Waits Chimes In" in her book, *Big Magic: Creative Living Beyond Fear*:

"… through watching his children create so freely, Waits had an epiphany: It [his work] wasn't actually that big a deal. He told me, 'I realized that, as a songwriter, the only thing I really do is make jewelry for the inside of other people's minds.' Music is nothing more than decoration for the imagination. That's all it is. That realization, Waits said, seemed to open things up for him. Songwriting became less painful after that."

"Intracranial jewelry-making! What a cool job!" exclaimed Liz Gilbert in the next paragraph of her book.

I completely agree. What we do is cool but not necessarily vital.

There are of course exceptions where books and other kinds of art have saved lives. Even for the smallest of us. Like, Juniper, a baby girl born in critical condition and placed in an incubator, whose breathing stabilized as her father read her the *Harry Potter* books, while the rest of the family surrounded her with love.*

But for the most of us, art is not necessary for survival.

This realization takes massive weight from one's shoulders. It took quite a few tons off of mine.

If I were a jewelry-maker, I wouldn't expect my creations to change someone's lives. I would just hope that people would find something they like out of what I had to offer. That is all. I am sure I would not be so naive as to think that *each* piece I created would be some talisman and that each talisman had to be bought and loved.

Yes, some jewelry is special and can be a talisman. And still, it's not something that will nurture and save you in a critical situation.

On the other hand, you as a customer expect a lot when you enter a jewelry shop. You expect to find something special – the best creations the jeweler has to offer. And you are most fascinated when you see that the creator of those small intricate works of art has put all of himself and his heart into them, and that each creation has a story.

Finding parallels between the jewelry example above and fiction writing is easy. But does this apply only to fiction?

I don't think so. Guide books are not important to our survival either, even if some of them do contain the phrase *survival guide* in their titles. Guide books are like those fancy knives with zig-zag edges, which are never described as essential, but cooking and styling your dinner becomes so much more fun with them. Or much faster, or much easier. But still, most people could do without them.

So why are those fiction and non-fiction books worth it if they are not essential for our immediate survival?

Maybe because we hope to create and offer something inspiring, enlightening, uplifting, and which helps ourselves and others enjoy this adventure called life.

As I was writing the article that served as the first draft for this chapter, one of my friends shared the following quote by G.D. Falksen with me on Facebook:

"Art is not necessary for life. Art is necessary for making life worth living."

This sentence brought goose-bumps tickling my arms as I perceived its utter truthfulness. *Harry Potter* books and her father's soothing voice reading them must have shown the little girl, Juniper, that life was worth living.

To create something for **"making life worth living"** is one of the highest missions in life one could imagine.

A call for action: Dear fellow writers, let's show each other the jewelry we create. Let's show each other what we've got. I'm sure we will find there something extraordinary for each other. Something we could never have found in our own worlds.

Best-selling authors and developers of Instantaneous Transformation, Ariel and Shya Kane, said something wonderful and truly revealing in this respect:

*"Each person's 'ordinary' is another's 'extraordinary'. Being one's self and sharing that with others is simply a gift."***

References in this chapter:

* http://www.upworthy.com/jk-rowling-found-out-her-books-helped-save-this-babys-life-her-response-was-magic

** *Practical Enlightenment*, Ariel and Shya Kane, 2015

T – Tell It Like It Is

We've talked about being honest with oneself while writing ("Introduction (Part 3) – What This Book is...and is Not About" as well as Chapter "A – Action") and editing (Chapter "E – Editing"). We've also talked about being "split open," as Natalie Goldberg says in her book, *Writing Down the Bones: Freeing the Writer Within* (Chapter "B – Book").

But what does it mean to be honest with oneself and other people? What does it mean to *tell it like it is*?

The answers might mean something different for each of us. But are there commonalities?

What I discovered surprised me immensely. I was astounded because the realizations were so new to me and also because, at the same time, they made so much sense.

Honesty and kindness are mutually inclusive and cannot be true without one another

For a long time, I erroneously thought that being kind to myself meant claiming time and space for myself away from others. Aspiring writers often hear, "Protect your writing time." Which makes it sound like somebody is attacking our writing time, or is eager to steal it. Sure, we get interrupted, but the same happens in every other job. In those jobs, even if we sometimes complain about interruptions, we try to go back to the task as soon as possible afterwards. Or we ask others not to disturb us for some time. But this complaint about the lack of time is so frequently mentioned when it comes to writing. At least, I have never heard interruptions spoken of more often or with a more negative tone than since I became a writer.

For me, the brightest lightbulb in this respect went off one evening when I complained to my husband about my lack of time for writing. "Other authors take one hour or more in the evenings to write, or even go to writers' retreats with the sole purpose of writing their books. I also want this! Even if it is just for five minutes every day."

His answer was short and couldn't have been more honest, direct and, I must admit, fair. He said, "So go to your desk, close the door behind you, and write."

I was speechless. All I could do in response was go to our little home office, shut the door, put the timer on for five minutes and write.

I managed to write three short paragraphs during those five minutes. I did edit them heavily later, but the ease with which they'd flowed struck me. I realized that the whole heaviness of the task didn't come from the lack of time to write but from the drama I had created around taking this time. The drama had not contained even an ounce either of kindness or honesty, neither to those around me nor myself.

I observed myself "testing" honesty and kindness towards myself and others, and tried to apply them separately, but I realized that they stopped existing without each other.

When I tried being kind to myself without seeing that I was the one preventing myself from doing what I wanted to do and instead trying to put the blame on others, I stopped being kind altogether. Blaming others for my inability to take time for my writing didn't buy me a ticket to feeling good as I thought it would. I thought that by putting the responsibility for this on others would relieve the guilt I felt inside. It didn't.

After that, I decided to blame myself instead, expose my "mistakes" (almost) publicly. That was my idea of being honest. But soon after, I felt miserable and started whining and asking people around me for mercy. To my surprise, many did have compassion and understanding. The one without compassion, who had been unable to see the truth, was me.

Grasping that honesty and kindness cannot fully bloom without each other was a big relief. There was suddenly both calmness and time to do what I wanted to do. I had neither to beat myself up nor to lie to myself. All there was to do was become aware that I was in discomfort, and then make a choice what to do next without trying to fix myself, anybody or anything. All there was to do was move forward. And people around me seemed not only to accept but also understand me more than they ever had before.

Ignorance is a way of saying *No* and being dishonest and unkind

Have you noticed that when you attempt to ignore someone or something, these people, things, events and memories seem to stick around? I experienced that at the first parents' meeting at my son's school in Fall 2016.

I was very much looking forward to this event. For two reasons. First, I had never been at a parents' and teachers' meeting at a school before, and as a kid I had always wondered what was happening there. All the accounts by my parents, my elder sister (who after our father's death attended the meetings instead of him), and movies, all the many kinds of possible and impossible scenarios they displayed couldn't replace the wish to experience them for myself. The parents' evenings in kindergarten didn't count, either. It simply had to be a first-hand experience at a school.

The second reason was that I was curious to see how they happened nowadays and especially in a country so different from the one I grew up in.

So even the planned two-and-a-half-hour duration couldn't stop my happy anticipation of the event. I volunteered to go and was very curious about it.

When I arrived, I saw many other parents gathering. Some of them also had older children in that school and knew the teachers and each other. Others were as new as I was.

I noticed that some of the parents seemed not too keen on being there. Or at least they weren't that merry or smiling. *Well, we all have our stories and 'fights' inside us. So, who knows why they aren't smiling,* I thought.

I decided to ignore them and concentrate on my positive anticipation, no matter who was smiling or not, no matter how many prejudices I had heard about parents' evenings, especially the lengthy ones – I'd been told that two and a half hours for a parents' meeting was way too long! So, I waited for the meeting to begin, watched the teachers, and tried to ignore the other parents.

At some point, I noticed that I wasn't smiling anymore, that I had a frown above my eyes and anxious thoughts filling my mind. *What if Niklas has done something wrong and they are going to speak about this today? In front of all other parents?! What if he was not coping with the school very well? What if the way we are educating him at home is wrong?*

These thoughts rushed in, even though the reality of how I had experienced my son since he started school was completely different. His posture had changed, his attitude also. He was helping more and more at home, had become calmer and positively thoughtful. He loved speaking of what he learned at school, looked forward to the next day and even asked me to let him stay longer at school after hours.

So why was I having those thoughts?

I didn't manage to answer that question in my head because I suddenly let myself observe the way those worrisome thoughts made me feel.

Then it dawned on me. *That was how the frowning parents felt!* They might not have had the exact same thoughts that I had, but those tightening arms of worry were most likely squeezing them in the same manner that they were squeezing me – fear, or at least anxiety, of what might come out at this meeting.

As I embraced this observation, instead of ignoring and rejecting it, I found my frown disappearing and started smiling again. But with a different kind of smile than before.

I found myself looking into other parents' eyes. And…they smiled back at me.

That was an amazing discovery. There and then, I understood that the same experience applied to all areas of my life, including writing.

When I tried to ignore my desire to write a book (see Chapter "B – Book"), the thoughts of it and of a specific story, that of my father, kept coming back. This battle inside my head was anything but pleasant. But everything changed as soon as I surrendered and embraced the idea of putting my dad's story into words.

Now, I practice embracing what comes my way more and more often. I can't stop being surprised and awed by how rich these experiences are.

Ignorance does not protect us from unwanted things. Disregarding people and events calling for our attention won't help because we are never isolated, not even when we are alone and feel lonely.

There are, of course, people, actions, and events that sometimes deserve to be said *No* to or deliberately ignored, including anyone or anything biased towards aggression. Because attackers and aggressors gain their energy and power from attention.

But if anyone or anything stirs something up inside us, then ignorance about how we and others feel will only hurt us and make us suffer more. The same way that ignoring a traffic sign can be fatal, ignoring a feeling generated by the world around us can make our lives poorer and more agonizing.

I learned from Ariel and Shya Kane and their transformational approach toward awareness and being in the moment, that the most enjoyable way to live life is to allow ourselves and others to:

- be the way we all are at any given moment,

- be present with mind and body in this given moment,

- see what is there to do without ignorance, judgment (acknowledging that ignorance is a form of judgment), evaluation, or any other bias,

- and do it.

You don't have to explain too much to come to the point. Fear has the tendency to "bend" the truth

Here comes our old friend fear again. Have you noticed that sometimes when you want to say something, you try to wrap it up inside a long introduction as if it was a fragile antique book or vase that you need to handle with special gloves?

We often forget that truth is solid and sharp, like a knife. Wrapping it up hides what it is about. I've observed that when I try to prepare my listener for the truth with a long introduction, I lose him or her. Then when my point comes, they don't get it. I get an impression that they've disagreed with or rejected me. Only after a lengthy clarification, do we find out that we were of the same opinion or that what I wanted to say resonated with them.

Of course, we need to be attentive to the way we present our truth to others so that it doesn't offend them. But we don't have to wrap it up in something thick and cumbersome in order for someone to get it. If we do, they might go right on by without noticing anything.

Let's go back to the analogy of a knife. If somebody asks you to pass them a knife, you will surely take care that the sharp side doesn't face their hand when they take it. At the same time, I am sure that you wouldn't pack the knife into a thick roll of paper, or those plastic wrappings with thousands of tiny airpockets, before handing it over.

"Telling it like it is" is the best path to take in fiction, too

"Well," you might ask, "this is all well and good for non-fiction, but aren't you supposed to imagine and fake things in fiction?"

Imagine — *Yes*. Fake — *No*.

Even the word *imagination* doesn't quite express the way the truth is said in fiction.

I see imagination as a transmission device and a door opener. We imagine, for example, "I'm on the moon, or in the Oval Office, or with Alice in Wonderland." Imagination brings us there. But the combination of all that we've learned growing up, with all of the knowledge we have now, plus the magic motor of our brains, causes us to see fiction with more clarity – it almost ceases to be fictional.

Take dreams for example. They come in pictures, especially the striking ones, leaving us, as we open our eyes, wondering whether we are awake or fell asleep.

I believe that the *"true"* fiction comes in surreal but vivid images. We look somewhere beyond the desk and computer screen we are working at, and see our characters and the scenes in which they are involved. Then we try to capture what we see in words. But if you take your attention off the scene and try to claim something is happening without actually witnessing or feeling it, then you are faking it, and the reader will know.

The first time I experienced such vivid imagery was when writing my first novel, *The Truth About Family*. In one scene, I was trying to figure out what could have made my dad, the protagonist, become oblivious of a person that had been bullying him for many years.

And so I imagined or rather "turned" to peer inside the headmaster's office, "made" all characters freeze and "entered" the room. I realized that my father was looking for something in particular, then tried to find the spot he was looking at. In the next moment, I saw what that was. A letter he had waited so long for and which he hoped would bring him news about his long-lost family.

I could clearly see the letter, in its thin, yellowish envelope with an address scribbled in spiky letters and black ink. The recipient's name was that of my father.

This description of the letter never found its way into the book, but seeing it helped me describe my dad's feelings upon discovering his name on the envelope, that the sender would be the one he hoped it to be.

In my initial attempts to describe the scene, before I "entered the room," I speculated that my father might have been ignoring the bully by sheer force of will, trying instead to concentrate on the headmaster. But all this felt strange and wasn't working. It was like I was recounting the story as told by a third person who had never been there.

"Entering" and "seeing" the room opened a whole new possibility and helped me feel what authenticity means while writing fiction.

No one can see a scene and the setting around it as I see them.

Another person would see them with different eyes. And this seeing – very personal to me – is what makes my writing original and true.

There are many perfect ways to tell it like it is. And that experience of perfection can change with time and based on what we learn

So now we know what to look for when telling it like it is. Whatever it is, we know exactly how to say it. There is only one way of doing it. Right?

Yes and *No*.

No, because you can write the same story, the same sentence, in various ways or from different points of view. Frustratingly (or maybe not so), they all have the ability to be true.

Even for the same person the truth can be different in various moments and situations.

Elizabeth Gilbert, author of *Eat, Pray, Love,* wrote the following about a 10-page-long short story, which she had to rewrite and shorten by 30% to be published in a magazine:

"The new version was neither better nor worse than the old version; it was just profoundly different."*

And I am sure both versions felt true to her in the moments they were created and polished.

So, *No,* there isn't one single way to tell it like it is.

But the answer is also *Yes.* Because there is only one choice at any given moment. We usually choose the one that feels better or right to us. This choice becomes our truth for that moment.

Other people might not believe that we mean what we say. But their belief or trust doesn't always have to do with us

If we tell the truth and bring our authentic selves into what we write, why then do some people not believe us? Why do they frown at what we write or what we say? Can it be that we didn't tell the truth, even if at that moment when the words were born we were sure of their authenticity?

One of the reasons for my fear of writing a book or sharing my writing in general, was the worry that other people wouldn't like it, and most of all I was afraid of being criticized and told that what I did wasn't correct, not right, not true.** That it was all wrong. Even if I gave all of me and did the very best I could.

Feeling my brows moving together, I used to think: *Why don't some people appreciate my writing, especially when I obviously need that appreciation the most?*

Well, the answer was both revealing and surprising. Individuals who criticize without any constructive ideas are worried too. Their critique often has little to do with me. It often reflects their own worries and fears, their struggle. It can also mean that what I have created has stirred something inside them, made them confused and uncomfortable.

Many of us have heard, in one way or another, sayings like:

- ***"The path to enlightenment goes through confusion"*** or

- ***"If you want to meet your true self then you need to step out of your comfort zone"***

But knowing those wise words doesn't always save us from upsets and negative reactions when something strikes that sensitive cord inside us.

When I experienced this new-to-me realization about why some people are so harsh in their critiques, I genuinely calmed down. Understanding that these people are just as vulnerable as I am, that they too are utterly scared of being critiqued and unappreciated just as I am at times, helped me relax and stop judging them.

Some words of conclusion about *telling it like it is*

I thought this chapter would be short. But it ended up being one of the longest in this book. Maybe because the meaning of telling the truth is paradoxical. It is both absolute and indefinite. Absolute and precise for one person, in his or her circumstance at one particular moment; different for other people and circumstances, varying over time. Our truth is not absolute over time. But it does feel absolute and lasting if we don't take other people's reactions to it personally, if we just let them go, and if we just come back to the current moment to find the truth of right here and right now.

A question for contemplation: What does telling the truth when writing mean for you right now as you finish reading this chapter?

References in this chapter:

* Elizabeth Gilbert, *Big Magic: Creative Living Beyond Fear*, Section "Trust," Chapter "Lighten Up"

** See more in the Chapter "L – Life, Libel, and Liability"

U – Uncertainty Principle (or Trying to Understand How It All Happens)

I have a rational mind or at least I used to think so for a very long time, even when it seemed to behave very irrationally at times.

This rational mind tries to understand and be sure about everything that I have to deal with.

Of course, it was and still is quite often utterly annoyed, confused, and scared when something unexpected happens that is impossible to grasp. When an event seems to have thousands of reasons. OK, if not thousands then at least a handful and not just one. Yes, my mind was and is often searching for one reason, one way, one exact definition. One choice.

We already saw that this is not possible. At least not over time. And this *over time* happens extremely fast. Moments occur in amounts of time much shorter than a second. How are we supposed to follow? How are we meant to know which choice to make or which direction to take?

During my time as a practicing physicist, and having dealt with physics on a very low scale (in other words having worked with atoms, electrons, waves and other fantastic matters), I learned about the *uncertainty principle* introduced by the German physicist Werner Heisenberg in 1927.

Here is one definition of the *uncertainty principle*:

"The Uncertainty principle is also called the Heisenberg uncertainty principle. Werner Heisenberg stumbled on a secret of the universe: No thing has a definite position, a definite trajectory, or a definite momentum. Trying to pin a thing down to one definite position will make its momentum less well pinned down, and vice-versa."*

In other words, when you try to identify one property of an electron, for example, you cannot precisely measure the other.

Wow! Can you see the relieving power of this principle?

If we apply this to our lives in general and to work in particular – to our writing, for example – then this principle could be reworded as follows:

When we choose one storyline or particular plot (for instance, our protagonist marries, dies, or comes back as an angel after death; but only one of these at a time), we will never be able to know for certain how the other possibilities could have developed.

And we will never be able to know whether the other options are better or not. Even if we give up the initial plot line and choose another. Because by abandoning the first one we stop "measuring it," we stop keeping our hand on its pulse and it stops existing.

Do you know why I believe this is true? Because we are made of atoms, electrons, particles, waves and all the other fantastic matters of this world, so we follow those laws of physics as a whole just like the tiny bits of us do.

A call for action: Let's stop worrying about whether another storyline or another take on what we have to say would be better or not. We cannot say for sure because we simply can't. Let's just concentrate on the choice we made and go on with it.

And if we choose to abandon this present idea at some point, then let's do it. It's another choice to make and we can only measure for sure what we have chosen, right here and right now. Nothing else.

References in this chapter:

*

https://simple.wikipedia.org/wiki/Uncertainty_principle

V – Voice

(Discovering It in Each Moment Rather Than Finding It)

This article might end up being one of the shortest in the book. That's because there is only one message to deliver, which is already reflected in its title. It is something I realized some time ago about a piece of writing advice I had heard many times, my perception of which – I realize now in retrospect – encouraged me to overthink the quality of my writing and even impeded my ability to just write.

This statement or advice is often given to aspiring writers. They are often told, "Find your voice."

They are also told to imitate, practice, try and try again until they find their voice.

What I experienced when trying to embrace and follow this advice were the thoughts: *What if I don't find my voice? What if it sounds like somebody else's?*

A strange thing happened when I sat down and wrote without much thinking. Just letting myself be led by the ignition of an idea, or an initial sentence given by an exercise or something from my imagination. Seemingly out of nowhere, words appeared. And there was a voice in the words I wrote.

Now I realize, each of us has a voice. Since the day we were born. This voice inside every one of us changes over time. I discovered that my voice is sometimes sad, sometimes merry, sometimes utterly strange, at times understanding and kind. Fortunately, it is rarely mean, aggressive or attacking in any way (although this type of voice is useful time to time, when making the antagonists talk).

As I let myself consider what made me uncomfortable with the advice of finding one's voice, I saw that I stumbled over the word *find*. Finding one's voice somehow sounds to me like the searching should be outside of oneself. But we have already a voice. We might not know it, but it is there. It's always been there.

Another problem I see with wanting to find something is the absoluteness of this statement. It sounds like if you find it, you have it and that's it. But a writer's voice is not static. Depending on the mood, on the genre, on the circumstances, that voice absorbs the external and internal world of a writer like a sponge, creating an incredible and always surprising cocktail of thoughts, emotions, and impressions.

So my advice to you and myself is to sit down, *just* write and let's discover our voices in the process. And *Yes*, read, go to the movies, talk to your loved ones and people you don't know, go for a walk, engage in stimulating discussions, enjoy your meals, and absorb all this. Absorb also what you feel inside at any given moment. Observe your feelings without judging them. And then sit down and write again, and again. And then some more.

After some time, pick up what you have written and read it. Discover your voice in that particular moment from the recent or long gone past. Experience the feelings generated by this reading, as well as the anticipation of new creations to come from the near or far-off future. This will lead you to a new shade of your voice in the present moment.

W – Wonder and How We Find Our Path to It

In the Chapter "I – Ideas and Inspiration," we talked at length about finding ideas and inspiration. The conclusion was that we couldn't control how the ideas appear. They can be anything and can appear anywhere. Completely unexpectedly.

That could be the clue. The unexpectedness of it all.

But where does the unexpected start? How do we find a way to the point where we exclaim or whisper, "Wow!"?

How do we locate the beginning of the path that leads to that moment when we are taken by the power of wonder and into the momentum of passion?

One of my favorite writers, who has been quoted many times in this book, Elizabeth Gilbert, wrote the following brilliant words in *Big Magic: Creative Living Beyond Fear*:

"I believe that curiosity is the secret. Curiosity is the truth and the way of creative living. Curiosity is the alpha and the omega, the beginning and the end. Furthermore, curiosity is accessible to everyone. Passion can seem intimidatingly out of reach at times – a distant

tower of flame, accessible only to geniuses and to those who are specially touched by God. But curiosity is a milder, quieter, more welcoming, and more democratic entity. The stakes of curiosity are also far lower than the stakes of passion. Passion makes you get divorced and sell all your possessions and shave your head and move to Nepal. Curiosity doesn't ask nearly so much of you.

In fact, curiosity only ever asks one simple question: 'Is there anything you're interested in?'

Anything?

Even a tiny bit?

No matter how mundane or small?"

Curiosity was what made Liz try out gardening. The gardening later made her curious about plants and their origins, and then about the history of botany, and finally ignited a passion for writing an epic story of a woman passionate about botany and discovering through botany the secrets of the world. Her novel, *The Signature Of All Things,* was an amazing best-selling work of creativity which, despite being fiction, was nominated in Great Britain in 2014 for The Welcome Prize, an award for achievement in writing on a medical subject. *The Signature of All Things,* or SOAT as Liz Gilbert loves referring to her now-famous novel, was the only fiction book on the list of nominees, alongside the works of recognized scientific authors like Andrew Solomon and Oliver Sachs.* I am sure this nomination was due to the amazingly meticulous research clearly visible when reading the novel.

Many would agree that such an achievement could not be possible without passion.

But the passion came later.

For her, and I dare to say for all of us, the magic of any passion starts with curiosity.

Curiosity was also what helped me to take my first steps in writing. My fear was too big to let me feel the looming passion for writing inside me. But curiosity was a gentle friend. "Don't worry. Just try it out. You don't have to commit to anything." It said, "Taste it and if you don't like it, spit it out."

After writing my first short story in 2009 in a notebook, which I later revised, had edited and published as an e-book on my website under the title *Between Grace and Abyss*, I didn't "spit" the writing out. I liked the taste too much. And I still love it to this day.

Yes, I am sure that curiosity, this gentle friend, will also help me out in other daunting beginnings and endings. "Let's see what we can do today," it will tell me.

A call for a continuous action: Let's continue our journey into the wonder of creativity, and start by looking around and looking closer when we say, either out loud or to ourselves, "Hm, this could be interesting."

References in this chapter:

* You can read about Liz's excitement on her nomination on her website by following this link: http://www.elizabethgilbert.com/so-honored-dear-ones-the-signature-of-all-things-has-been-nominated-for-a/.

X – X-ing Out

(or How To Face Self-Edits)

In the Chapter "E – Editing," we talked about the process of editing and what emotions might rush through us when opening a file sent to us by our editor with our revised manuscript.

Some time ago, I found myself struggling with self-edits. As I wrote this chapter, I was also in the process of incorporating the second round of self-edits into *Take Control of Your Business*, my book on business rules* mainly targeted at small businesses.

The self-edits on paper went easily on some days and a bit slower on others. But they didn't stagnate for more than a few days in a row. However, when incorporating them into the manuscript on my computer, they did. For more than three days in a row.

The reason appeared to be simple. The pages were full of hand-made notes. On some pages, it seemed that changes needed to be made multiple times on every row. Additionally, I realized that two chapters had to switch places. That would mean at least some modifications of

                    Victoria Ichizli-Bartels

the text inside those chapters, as well as those adjacent to them.

I didn't expect so much change to come in the second self-edit. I thought things like that happened in the first self-edit, not the second. Looking back, I am not quite sure which of the self-edits was harder for my previous books, but my brain had the idea that self-edits would gradually become easier with each new edit. I was wrong. At least for this non-fiction book.

Was that false expectation the reason for my procrastination? I don't know now, I didn't know it at that time, and it probably doesn't matter at all.

What mattered was how to move forward from there.

Inspired by my "gamified" style of working – my notebook of to-do lists carries the name "Victoria's Game Book" – I came up with the following idea. *Why don't I give myself one point for each change I implement, whether it is a deletion, insertion, replacement, or a combination of all three, and see how many points I can "win"?* I thought. *This will allow me to concentrate on each step since points can only be gathered one by one in this case. While working on one of the changes, I might forget about the daunting appearance of the whole project and just be busy winning those points.*

I can report now that this approach worked. At some point, I stopped counting a point for each edit, and incorporating changes went smoothly from there. Ultimately, this method let me step over my procrastination and reclaim fun in working on every stage of the project.

I read recently that playing games at work can be very motivating but also has some negative by-products. One of these adverse side effects is the apparent decrease in productivity after the motivating game has finished.

But what if we don't stop playing? What if we take every step in the projects we pursue as if it were a move or turn in a strategic game?

Do you remember the famous quote by George Bernard Shaw?

"We don't stop playing because we grow old; we grow old because we stop playing."

We don't have to stop playing at all. Life is a fun game. Let's play it. Let's stay young.

Each project has, of course, its rules, and we are the game designers who develop and adjust them. The main adjustment we have to make is how to bring the fun factor** into the project to be carried out. And remember, we are also the customers, the players of these games we design and develop.

Gathering as many points as I can for a given project is great fun for me. Once, by addressing many small and urgent tasks, I managed to collect fifteen points in a day. I felt elated by the end of the day when I looked at my notepad and tallied up my score.

Now I am off to my next project-game for today, which happens to be some of the self-editing work I mentioned above. But using my playful point-gathering approach I predict that there is a good chance of finishing this project, and having fun with a task I had previously found daunting.

A question to you: What's your next project-game?

References in this chapter:

* *"Business rules are about products. They are the rules a company and its partners, and to some extent also its customers, need to agree upon and follow for the products and services to be of high quality and longevity."* *Take Control of Your Business: Learn what Business Rules are, discover that you are already using them, then update them to maximize your business success,* Victoria Ichizli-Bartels, 2017

** See also Chapter "H – Hook (or the Fun-Detecting Antenna)"

Y – Yearning and Yawning (or the Alleged Yo-yo Effect of Curiosity)

Here is one of the dialogues I had with myself about the powers that inspire us and bring us to places we never expected to visit before daring to jump into the ocean of creativity.

"Passion, curiosity, searching and keeping an open mind for wonders, all these help us wake up in the morning and step into our days with enthusiasm." The worrying me drew her brows together despite the positive statement she just made.

She seemed to need this facial movement to let her fully express what she was going to say next. "But what about those moments when we yawn, when we have had enough, and need a nap or another kind of break from our curiosity-driven natures?" she asked.

"What about them?" the laid-back me raised her brows.

"Do they bring us right back to where we were at the beginning, just like a yo-yo does after reaching the top?"

"I don't think so."

"But it does feel like that sometimes!" The worried me pulled her shoulders up. "We are often exhausted after reaching the top. All that elation lasts maybe a second, and then, Boom! The head is empty again. Aren't we supposed to keep moving forward?"

"Hm, it's a good question." The laid-back me leaned back in her chair and put her hand around the espresso cup standing on the table in front of her.

"I know!" The worried me pitched forward and seemed to want to crawl into my computer in an attempt to make the things go faster.

The laid-back me sipped her coffee and said, "I have an idea. What if creativity and the achievements connected with it are like a great cup of coffee? What if after drinking it up, you feel so wonderful that you are already looking forward to the next one. That is the next step you've been talking about."

She took another sip and continued. "Yet, you are aware that the coffee in a dirty cup with cold coffee stains won't be as good as the one you just had. So, you go and wash the cup. That is what the elation and euphoria about your achievement do. They wash and free your mind for the next portion of the creative challenge. You are like the cup, and before you can have another refill, you need to dry up and get warm again to be ready for the next portion of coffee." The laid-back me finished her espresso and stood up to wash her cup.

The worried me opened her eyes wide and noticed herself leaning back in her chair, her shoulders releasing, her wrinkled brows softening.

Epilogue

Yawning is not an enemy of yearning to be creative. It is rather its partner, making sure that we get a break, get "washed," warm and ready for the next creative leap forward.

P.S.

The word *yawn* became one of my favorite words after I read, at the age of 24, a sweet tale in German, where a baby yawned and in a chain-reaction caused the whole world to yawn, which according to the author was a good thing because on this day everyone went early to bed. That was the very first story I read in full in the German language and it immediately became one of my favorites. Previously, I had thought of yawning as something unnecessary, unpleasant to see or even annoying. After reading this story, which made me smile and feel unexpectedly and extremely happy, I now enjoy when people yawn around me. I yawn with them, smile at this mysterious social phenomenon, and take a break.

Z – Zeal

This is the last chapter in *Cheerleading for Writers: Discover How Truly Talented You Are.* I hope you enjoyed this collection of articles. It was a joy for me to write them. Writing this book boosted my energy to work on my other projects.

For this last article, I have chosen the word *zeal.*

Here is how Oxford Dictionaries defines it:

*"Great energy or enthusiasm in pursuit of a cause or an objective."**

And I think there is no better word to end this book with.

Because this is what *cheerleading* is for: to motivate us in finding, discovering, and storing this great energy and enthusiasm in pursuit of what we love to do.

I hope the articles in this book made you smile, helped you see how powerful and amazingly creative you are. And especially, how unique! There is no one like you, and no one can write your stories as you do. Only YOU can. Even somebody else's stories – like fairy tales – if you tell them and put your perspective, your feelings, your thoughts into your retelling of them, these stories will be entirely different. They will become *your* stories.

So, go on, soak up the life, its stories, its colors, take it all in, experience it, and share with the world how you see and perceive it.

The light radiating through your prism of seeing and feeling is one of a kind.

Happy, happy writing, dear writer-friends!

References in this chapter:

* https://en.oxforddictionaries.com/definition/zeal

Recommended Reading

1. *Being Here: Modern Day Tales of Enlightenment*, Ariel and Shya Kane, 2007

2. *Practical Enlightenment*, Ariel and Shya Kane, 2015

3. *Working on Yourself Doesn't Work: The Three Simple Ideas That Will Instantaneously Transform Your Life*, Ariel and Shya Kane, 2008

4. *Writing Down the Bones: Freeing the Writer Within*, Natalie Goldberg, 2010

5. *Big Magic: Creative Living Beyond Fear*, Elizabeth Gilbert, 2015

6. *Creative Writing: A Guide and Glossary to Fiction Writing*, Colin Bulman, 2006

7. *Bird by Bird: Some Instructions on Writing and Life*, Anne Lamott, 1995

8. *Writing Affirmations: A Collection of Positive Messages to Inspire Writers*, Rob Bignell, 2014

9. *Chicken Soup for the Soul: Inspiration for Writers: 101 Motivational Stories for Writers – Budding or Bestselling – from Books to Blogs*, by Jack Canfield, Mark Victor Hansen, Amy Newmark, and Susan M. Heim, 2013

10. *On Writing: 10th Anniversary Edition: A Memoir of the Craft,* Stephen King, 2010

11. *How to Make a Living as a Writer,* James Scott Bell, 2014

12. *Business For Authors. How To Be An Author Entrepreneur,* Joanna Penn, 2014

13. *How to Write Dazzling Dialogue: The Fastest Way to Improve Any Manuscript,* James Scott Bell, 2014

14. *The Emotion Thesaurus: A Writer's Guide to Character Expression,* as well as other Thesauri for writers by Angela Ackerman & Becca Puglisi, 2012

15. *Creating Unforgettable Characters: A practical guide to character development in: films, TV series, advertisements, novels & short stories,* Linda Seger, 1990

16. *Outlining Your Novel: Map Your Way to Success,* K.M. Weiland, 2011

17. *Captivate Your Readers: An Editor's Guide to Writing Compelling Fiction,* Jodie Renner, 2015

18. *How to Fix Your Novel: Simple techniques to improve your manuscript and get it published,* Steve Alcorn, 2012

19. *Editor-Proof Your Writing: 21 Steps to the Clear Prose Publishers and Agents Crave,* Don McNair, 2013

Acknowledgements

The first person I would like to thank here is the person who inspired the creation of this book. It is my dear friend, Marcy, Marcella Belson. You inspired both the idea and the title of this book and are one of my biggest and most cherished cheerleaders. Thank you for being my friend and supporting me, especially through my first years of becoming a professional writer. I will never forget how we met on the internet and how our friendship developed. And I will always look forward to our monthly telephone calls. You will always be in my heart, Marcy, and I am immensely grateful to know you, even if, as I write these words, we haven't met in person yet. Who knows? This little book might even help us meet in person for the first time and give each other a big, big hug.

There are many people without whom I most probably wouldn't have become a writer, and had I not met them, you wouldn't have read this book. Two of these people are Ariel and Shya Kane, whose book, *Being Here: Modern Day Tales of Enlightenment*, captivated me first with its cover, then its content, and then its authors, who are immensely inspiring and who have become for me very, very dear friends. They give the gift of awareness, kindness, being well in oneself, and living life to its fullest to all who attend their seminars, listen to their radio shows, read their books and follow them on social media. I am immensely grateful to you, dear Ariel and Shya, for showing me and many of your friends all over the world, how fun and beautiful life can be, if we are simply there for it.

There are many writers I have learned from, by reading their books, blog posts and articles. And also by learning from them in-person or over the phone, as in the case of my dear friend and best-selling author, Menna van Praag. Thank you so much for all you do, dear Menna, and for your friendship! Further, I would like to thank all writers at the Kill Zone Blog for the wisdom they share every day, and especially James Scott Bell for all the great books on writing he creates and shares. I would also like to thank Angela Ackerman and Becca Puglisi for the brilliant resources you offer to writers. *The Emotion Thesaurus* is my best friend during the self-edits of my fiction. And thank you for the fun book launches you organize, one of which I had the great honor to take part in 2016. And finally, many thanks to Elizabeth Gilbert and Natalie Goldberg for writing some of the most inspiring books on writing.

I am incredibly grateful to my editor Leah Schneeflock, for making this book so much more readable and pleasant to read. This book is the second project we have worked on together, and I hope there are many more to come. It is an immense pleasure working with you, Leah!

I have to thank two of my dear friends for the beautiful book cover. Katrin Bauck for the unique art she created and Alice Jago for turning a piece of art into a book cover I treasure. Katrin, I fell in love with this painting as soon as I saw a photo of it. Thank you so much for allowing me to use it for *Cheerleading for Writers*! Alice, thank you so much for creating something so special every time we work together. Those little cheerleaders are magic!

Many thanks to my friends from the Black Label Writers' Club in Aalborg, Tammy Lain and Jesper Veiby, for listening to and reading some of the chapters of this book and providing valuable feedback. Seeing that you, as experienced writers, found value in it reassured me that other writers would find value in it too. And thank you very much for helping me to adjust the title of the book. I like it so much better now!

When I posted the last article from the blog series bearing the same name as this book, my sister-in-law, Jessica Bartels, or Jezz, as most in the family call her, posted the following comment about it in German, "Ich mag deinen Blog," which means "I like your blog." Dear Jezz, thank you for reading my books and blog posts and giving me encouraging feedback. And here in Denmark, I have a dear friend Antonia Krummheuer, who does the same for me as Jezz, reading my books and cheering me on with each achievement. Thank you so much to both of you, Jezz and Antonia, for your honest feedback and pointing to me your favorite bits in my books.

Three women in my life supported me in all my beginnings, and they know me like no other, now and long before my writing life. These are my mother, Veronica Ichizli, my sister, Svetlana Breum, and my niece, Mihaela Breum. You are the best, even if you might argue with that. Remember, I am taller. ;)

The biggest thanks go to my husband Michael, and my sweet children Niklas and Emma. Your love is incomparable, and it is an incredible source of creative power for me! I love you!

Let Me Know What You Think

Dear reader, dear writer,

Thank you very much for purchasing and reading *Cheerleading for Writers: Discover How Truly Talented You Are!*

I hope you enjoyed reading it.

If it stirred you in any way, I would like to ask you to take a moment and leave an honest review of this book on the retailer site where you purchased it. You can find the list of retailers offering it for sale on the webpage for *Cheerleading for Writers* (http://victoriaichizlibartels.com/cheerleading-for-writers/).

If you are a member of Goodreads, then a review there would be greatly appreciated as well.

Your feedback will help me grow as a writer, and it will help other potential readers discover this book.

Thank you very much for your help!

Please also take a moment to sign up for one or more of my blogs and occasional email updates. You'll then be the first to know about new content on the topics addressed in this book, as well as my book releases, special offers and other material. In addition, you will get two of my e-books for free (one short fiction story and one non-fiction guide to help you resolve tricky projects). You can unsubscribe at any time. To sign up, visit http://victoriaichizlibartels.com/subscribe-to-victorias-blog/. Thank you very much again!

If you like, you can reach me through one of the following:

- to my email Inbox: vib@optimistwriter.com

- via LinkedIn: dk.linkedin.com/in/victoriaichizlibartels/

- on Facebook: https://www.facebook.com/optimistwriter/

- on Twitter: https://twitter.com/VicaOw

I would love to hear from you!

About the Author

Victoria Ichizli-Bartels is a writer and specialist in the business development, information technology, semiconductor physics, and electronic engineering. She is the founder of Optimist Writer, writing, publishing and consulting business. She grew up in Moldova, lived in Germany for twelve years, and now lives in Aalborg, Denmark, with her husband and two children. Since 2015 Victoria has published an array of books, both fiction and non-fiction. Before that, she authored a Ph.D. thesis and many other scientific and technical publications.

Victoria has given various seminars and coaching sessions on fiction and creative non-fiction to aspiring writers in Aalborg, among other, at the South Gate Society School of Creating Writing, Aalborg, Denmark.

Visit Victoria at

victoriaichizlibartels.com

or

optimistwriter.com

Other books by Victoria

Fiction
The Truth About Family:
A novel inspired by true events

A Spy's Daughter:
A novella
(Book 1 in series "A Life Upside Down")

Seven Broken Pieces:
A short story
(Prequel to series "A Life Upside Down")

Nothing Is As It Seems: A Novelette
(The e-book is permanently free)

Between Grace And Abyss
(Available for free upon subscription to
victoriaichizlibartels.com)

Motivation

Turn Your No Into Yes:
15 Yes-Or-No Questions to Disentangle Your Project
(Available for free upon subscription to
victoriaichizlibartels.com)

5 Minute Perseverance Game:
Play Daily for a Month and Become the Ultimate
Procrastination Breaker

Business and Technology

S1000D Issue 4.1 Untangled:
552+ Business Rules Decision Points Arranged into a
Linear Topic Map to Facilitate Learning, Understanding
and Implementation of S1000D

Take Control of Your Business:
Learn what Business Rules are, discover that you are
already using them, then update them to maximize your
business success

S1000D® Issue 4.1 and Issue 4.2 Navigation Map:
552+87 and 427+90 Business Rules Decision Points
Arranged into two Linear Topic Maps to Facilitate
Learning, Understanding, and Implementation of
S1000D®